Hi, Beanie Chefs!

...à Mo... ...

Kid Beanie™

Table of Contents

Food Riddles 6	New May Beanies 25
10 Silliest Beanies 7	New Teenie Beanies 42
Miss "Beanie" Arizona 11	Complete Collection 49
Beanie Baby Day 12	Beanie Recipes 69
Roller Skating Into Olympics 13	Educational Cooking Games 192
Les & Sue Fox In Forbes 16	Beanie Birthdays 212
Beanie Tags 21	Collector's Checklist 214
Bongo & Congo Art Contest . 22	Answer Page 216

Professor Beanie™

Professor Beanie's
FOOD RIDDLES

(We've added a dash of humor and a pinch of goofy.)

1. Why did Pouch the Kangaroo order an extra portion of french fries?

2. Which Beanie Baby has a "walnut" tattoo on his forehead?

3. Name the favorite candy of Jolly The Walrus.

4. Who pours Tabasco sauce on his rice? (Please don't guess Tabasco!)

5. Why did Pinchers refuse to eat in a fancy restaurant with Digger and Claude?

6. When Roary The Lion devours a large T-Bone, who's seated to his left and right?

7. Which Beanie Baby eats more peanut butter? Congo or Blackie?

8. What do you feed blue Lizzy to turn her back into tie-dyed Lizzy?

9. Why does Steg fold his napkin into a perfect bow?

10. Who does Mystic The Unicorn sit across from at the breakfast table?

(Answers on page 216)

WORLD'S 10 SILLIEST BEANIES

BY LES & SUE FOX

© 1998 Artist: Diana Links

Fruit & Vegetable Beanies

Alice The Avocado™
An avocado a day
Is the Beanie Lover's way!

Bunch The Broccoli™
Broccoli is good for you
You can learn to love it, too!

Carol The Carrot™

Carol says carrots are good for
your eyes
Eat 'em and stare, you might get
a surprise!

Deena The Delicious Apple™
There is more than one kind of
apple, you know
Expand the possibilities and watch
your mind grow!

Edith The Eggplant™
The purple Beanie always wins
Because she's full of vitamins!

**Freddie The French-
Fried Zucchini™**

He's healthy as the day is long
Inside your stomach he belongs!

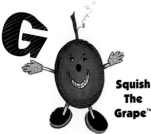

Squish The Grape™

Don't step on Squish
Cause she's delish!

Henry The Honeydew™
This honeydew is ripe with hope
The brother of a cantaloupe!

Irene The Irish Potato™

Irene's in town
So wolf her down!

Jamie The Jersey Tomato™
This "veggie" is a real life fruit,
Whatever you call her, Jamie's cute!

Help Roary & Friends Find the Hidden Objects

BEANIE BABIES ARE HERE TO STAY!

F ads come, and fads go. Pet rocks, Hula Hoops, tiny Troll-like toys with Don King Hairdos. The dictionary defines a fad as "an interest followed for a time with exaggerated zeal." The question is: Are Beanie Babies a fad? Or, if not, what are they? Are Beanie Babies truly "here to stay" as we have proclaimed in our books and music?

What gives a "fad" the staying power to evolve into a "hobby" like stamp collecting, or even an "institution" like baseball? Why do millions of "fans" continue to swarm into baseball stadiums to see the same eighteen grown men throw and hit the same baseballs they've been playing with since Abner Doubleday invented the game a century ago? Why do families keep tossing dice across the Monopoly board 60 years after the Great Depression? How many times can it really be "fun" to pass "Go" and collect $200? What's so exciting about watching your dad's face when he lands on your Boardwalk or Park Place with a hotel? (Admit it! You love to watch him squirm to avoid bankruptcy!)

The list of "permanent fads" is relatively short compared to the list of fads that died. However, all of the items on the short list have something in common. From Barbie Dolls, to Lionel trains to Scrabble, to professional sports, to Elvis Presley music, to birthday parties, "permanent fads" differ from short-term crazes in one important aspect. They're always fresh, new and exciting...and, they continue to "re-invent" themselves. Baseball games are actually like snowflakes. No two are exactly alike. Those "same" eighteen men change a little every game, and change completely every 10 or 15 years. Even baseballs have changed! People still love to compare every great new home run hitter to Mickey Mantle, Hank Aaron or Babe Ruth, every hotshot pitcher to Sandy Koufax, Whitey Ford or Satchel Paige. The truth is, to diehard fans, each and every game of baseball is a brand new experience. Just like every new game of Monopoly, every Barbie Doll, every Lionel Train. Some people hear something new each time they listen to "You Ain't Nothin' But A Hound Dog!"

Are Beanie Babies a passing fancy? We've said it before and we'll say it again: No way, José! Beanie Babies are more fun than a barrel of boring pet rocks. Ty constantly keeps us guessing what will happen next. He never fails to stimulate and satisfy us with an array of beautiful, exotic and affordable new toys every few months...just when we start to feel the craving for something new and different! If Beanie Babies turn out to be just another fad, I'll eat my hat. No, make that my 60th Anniversary Monopoly set: the Limited Edition "Star Wars" version with collectible coins!

By the way, who's been checking out all those snowflakes for duplicates?

Les & Sue Fox

BEANIE BABY BULLETIN #1

Miss Arizona
Is Also "Miss Beanie Baby!"

Photo by Tom Berry / Ford Studio

Meet Selly Straight, Miss Arizona 1998. Born and raised in Iowa she now resides in Tempe, Arizona. Selly says her unusual first name originated with a Hawaiian Princess (no, Ty is not re-naming the Princess Beanie Baby "Selly"), but has yet to discover the source of her equally interesting last name.

As you can see, Miss Arizona is slightly infatuated with Beanie Babies. Her collection numbers 104, and growing! Thanks to The Beanie Baby Handbook, she is able to keep track of which ones are easy to find and which are rare. "My ultimate goal is a complete collection." (Good luck!) A lover of dogs and stuffed animals (the perfect combination), Selly's first Beanie Baby purchase was a cute puppy named Bones. She recalls that on that same day oodles of Lefty's and Righty's were sitting happily on the shelf at only $5 apiece. "I should have bought them all before they started flying out the door!" she laments. But Miss "A" is still upbeat. "Beanie Babies are fantastic! Lots of people can afford to collect 100, and I just can't see an end to the craze. We all go wild with anticipation when new releases are announced."

A graduate of Arizona State University with honors in Marketing, Selly Straight has been a winner all of her life. She's the former Miss Junior Iowa and Miss Iowa Teen, and she plans on winning the Miss American United States pageant this fall. Selly's love for animals is a big reason why she loves Beanie Babies. She's an advocate of animal rights and would like to support this cause in a bigger way someday. As she plans her bright future (Selly's engaged), Selly pursues acting and modeling. She's done commercials and TV shows and worked on the set of Oliver Stone's "U-Turn." But every chance she gets, she hunts for more Beanies. (Like the rest of us.) "I also love Sheltie puppies," she confides. "I have two: Macy and Cacy. If Ty is listening, maybe he'll consider making Selly the Sheltie." Like they say, dreams are the stuff plush toys are made of...or something like that.

BEANIE BABY BULLETIN #2

First Beanie Baby Day At Yankee Stadium Goes Down in Baseball History!

The date is May 17, 1998, an overcast, slightly chilly afternoon. A crowd of 49,000 shows up for what promises to be a great Beanie Baby event highlighting "just another Yankees-Twins game." The Bronx Bombers bring out starting pitcher David Wells. He retires the first six batters in a row. Fans are playing with their free Valentinos. Some kids are trading their Valentino cards for a $5 bill. Here and there a dropped trading card lies underfoot, an extra bonus for those with good eyesight and quick reflexes.

Les and Jamie Fox are in the left field stands. They're joined by Les' longtime friend, ex-New York police officer Bob Brandes and Jamie's dinosaur-loving pal, Justin Roese. After a few warm hot dogs and super-size pretzels, and obtaining the Beanie prizes they came for, the so-so game seems unimportant. The Yanks are winning. Every few minutes a giant screen silently announces the winner of a special Beanie Baby. Jamie and Justin have better things to do back in New Jersey. So the foursome departs after the second inning. They beat the traffic.

Two hours later, the game is history. David Wells has pitched one of baseball's 15 "perfect games." His baseball cap, game ball and Valentino will go into The Baseball Hall Of Fame in Cooperstown! Beanie Baby Day at Yankee Stadium turns out to be more than just an interesting Sunday outing. Regrettably, Valentino The Bear was not specially marked. However, word is out that Valentino's serially numbered card is fetching $100 to $500! (NOTE: The 1999 Beanie Baby Handbook will cover "Beanie Baby Day" collectibles in depth.)

As a footnote, our "Beanie Baby Songs" have been played at several Beanie Baby baseball games, including St. Louis and Arizona. Take me out to the ball game! Take me out to the Beanie Baby crowd!

Beanie Babies Keep 'Em Rolling Toward Future Olympics

Pensacola, FL August 1997

Coach Debbie Lewis and National Gold Medal roller skater Jennifer Bland.

Did you know that Gold Medalist Tara Lipinski, darling of the 1998 Winter Olympics, started out as a competitive roller skater? I've learned a lot about the two skating disciples (roller and ice) since my 7-year old daughter, Jamie, became an avid roller skater. Every Saturday morning, after home-made pancakes, we head for *Skater's World* in Wayne, New Jersey. Brightly flashing multi-colored lights glisten off a polished oak floor clean enough to eat off. It is here that Sue and I spend at least three hours chatting, research-ing, writing on a laptop computer while Jamie hones her craft. It is unlikely that Jamie will seek to be a world champion. More importantly, she's getting good exercise, and learning to improve herself. Plus meet-ing friends who also enjoy rolling and spinning on skates or blades in a sleek balanc-ing act.

Does it really matter that none of these children can ever compete in the International Olympics? Probably not. Most seem happy enough just having fun on the weekend. However, for some kids roller skating is more serious. Members of the "Wayne Artistic Skating Club" (a team of 16 girls ages 5 to 14 - boys welcome, too!) aspire to greater glory. The best have gone all the way to "the nationals." In fact, Jamie's coach, Debbie Lewis, 27, (a skater since age 8) has already guided her stu-dents to 7 national gold medals. Today, the ultimate "win" for a roller skater (speed, artistic or hockey) is the Pan American Games, sanctioned by the U.S. Olympic Committee but not the International Olympic Committee. Unfortunately, roller skat-ing is not an international Olympic event, although speed skating could "break the ice" in the 2004 Olympics.

Like many frustrated roller skaters who'd like to elevate the public image of roller skating beyond sidewalk antics and the idiotic roller derby, Beanie Baby collectors Debbie and fiance Greg Caroselli, 26, have dedicated their young lives to the sport. Hoping to make this a lifetime career, they train amateur hopefuls to master the skills needed to make it to the top. Technique, timing and temperament all contribute to one's chances for success. But the price of success is not cheap. Private and group lessons (Debbie's sole source of income) earn her $15 to $30 an hour. Combined with Greg's limited income (due to a shoulder injury), they manage to pay the bills and have something left over for sports competition. Minor events set them back a couple of hundred bucks, plus parents' contributions. But the nationals are a different story.

Attending the U.S. Roller Skating National Championships (held in Fresno California in 1998) is a $20,000 affair. And that required a little creative fundraising. This year, Beanie Babies helped pay the bills.

On July 13, 1998, at the Wayne roller rink, some 300 people showed up for a special skating exhibition ("Family Fun Night") by Deb and Greg's present and future champions. Along with the show, which took in $2,800, the two coaches offered spectators a chance to help defray the cost of attending the nationals while adding to their Beanie Baby collections. (Deb says their own collection currently includes 130 toys. Their favorites are Stretch, Bongo and Hissy.) With the help of a few friends, including the authors of the Beanie Baby Handbook, the roller-skating Beanie auction (which included Princess and several retireds) realized a total of $1,000. Les and Sue Fox also made a cash contribution.

Olympics Maple helps special kids become sports champions.

Beanie Baby fundraisers are nothing new. Newspapers and magazines constantly report that Beanie Babies have helped raise money for hospitals, very sick kids and other worthy causes. It is estimated that Beanie Babies have funneled more than $20 million into the hands of those who need it most. Ty, Inc. alone has reportedly donated $2 million to The Princess Diana Memorial Fund. Ty's "Special Olympics" Maple Beanie Baby (a Canadian exclusive) has also been a significant source of public assistance. As time passes, more and more people will be helped by Beanie Babies. By the way, every member of the Wayne Artistic Skating Club is a Beanie Baby collector, including Jennifer Bland of New Milford, New Jersey, the team's first national champion.

Sadly, no matter how much money Beanie Babies help raise for charity and children's events, Jennifer Bland will still be shut out of Olympic competition. It is highly doubtful that she'll get a shot in 2004. Even if speed skating is admitted in 6 years (Jennifer's last chance), that won't help. Jennifer has won her national gold medals for artistic skating (freestyle and figures), which won't be considered until 2008. So the odds are slim that Jennifer will be able to tell her own kids how she made it to the Olympics.

Because McDonald's is an official Olympic Supporter (as well as the source of America's humongously popular "Teenie Beanie Babies"), we've taken our case to Brad Bell, Senior Marketing Vice President of the mega-corporation. Support from McDonald's would give the campaign for Olympic roller skating a needed shot in the arm. If you'd like to encourage Mr.Bell to join our cause, please write to him c/o McDonald's Corp., Oak Brook, IL 60521. Also write to the Editor of Sports Illustrated at: The Time-Life Building, New York, NY 10020. A major story in S.I. would greatly heighten public interest and make other powerful people aware of this situation.

Before giving you our latest "Hot Beanie Tips", please indulge us with a brief explanation of why roller skating is not, *but should be,* in the Olympics.

The U.S. Amateur Confederation of Roller Skating has been fighting to include their sport in the Olympics since the 1940's. The National Museum of Roller Skating (located in Lincoln, Nebraska) publishes a great book titled "The History Of Roller Skating", available at your local library. Did you know that the first in-line roller skate (the predecessor of "roller blades") was patented in 1819? In 1863, the first four-wheeled roller skate was invented by James L. Plimpton, a New York City furniture maker. In 1866, Plimpton's New York Roller Skating Association leased the Atlantic House, a Newport, Rhode Island hotel, and converted the dining room into a skating area! The first two roller rinks opened in 1876 in Paris and Berlin.

Today, roller skating (and blading) is at least 10 times as popular as ice-skating. One reason is that kids (and adults) simply can't ice-skate in the street. Among America's 2,600 rinks, three out of four are roller rinks, which are more profitable than expensive-to-operate ice rinks. That's why a 1-hour roller skating lesson runs only $30 compared to $60 for ice-skating. Roller hockey is one of the fastest growing sports in the country. Yet despite all of this history, popularity and economic benefit, only ice-skating gets the nod by the International Olympic Committee. Why? World class roller skaters like American Eric Anderson can perform all the same moves as ice skaters, including quadruple jumps. Last October, Anderson won a gold medal in the (non-Olympic) World Roller Skating Championships held in Spain. But you'll probably never see him perform.

The answer is simple, and perplexing. Only 10,000 athletes can compete in the Summer Olympics, and the events have reached their limit! In order to admit new sports, old ones have to be retired, like Beanie Babies. Due to politics and red tape, many existing sports have actually been expanded, keeping roller skating near the top of a long list of "Olympic Hopefuls." That's why 9 out of 10 talented roller skaters, like Tara Lipinski, switch to ice skating. By the time roller skating makes it to the Olympics, they'll be "over the hill." If you'd like to see things change, please write to McDonald's and Sports Illustrated and mention this story. For more information write to us at: West Highland Publishing, P.O. Box 36, Midland Park, NJ 07432.

And now for our hot tips. Here are some of the Beanies we see retiring in 1998: Strut, Rainbow, Snip (or maybe Chip), Chocolate, Wise and Snort. Get 'em while they're hot! (and cheap.) If you've got money, we also highly recommend buying a *genuine Olympic* Maple for around $400 (only twice the price of the regular Maple.) We predict that this toy (and the others listed above) could *triple in value within* two years!

Can you get rich collecting Beanie Babies? A new investment guide is hotter than the toys.

Feeding a fever

By Scott McCormack

AFTER 15 YEARS of a rising stock market, getting rich is getting to seem easy. The number two book on the *New York Times* how-to paperback bestseller list is—no, we're not kidding—*The Beanie Baby Handbook*. This opus suggests that all those pint-size stuffed animals will actually be worth something in a decade—thousands of dollars, if it is to be believed.

Clever move by authors Leslie and Sue Fox, a Wyckoff, N.J. husband-and-wife team, to cash in on one of the very biggest toy manias of the last two years (FORBES, *Oct. 21, 1996*). There are dozens of Internet sites, not to mention toy magazines, devoted exclusively to helping people build and unload their Beanie Babies collections. The shrewd toymaker, Oak Brook, Ill.-based Ty Inc., fuels the frenzy by periodically retiring old characters, which can inflate the price of $5 toys into four figures.

It's nothing like the tulip-bulb craze of 17th-century Holland yet, but we're making progress in that direction.

The Foxes' handbook poses as an "investment guide" to Beanie Babies, with "guesses" of the toys' values in the year 2008. Consider Peanut, a dark blue elephant, which sold for $5 in 1995. Ty won't disclose sales figures, but the Foxes claim that only 2,000 were made. Desperate collectors have paid up to $5,200 for the pachyderm. The Foxes estimate the price could go to $7,500 a decade from now.

Time to come clean. Les Fox, who once made a living

peddling silver dollars, has a personal stake. He estimates he owns almost $100,000 worth of Beanie Babies (a complete collection), and surely wouldn't mind seeing their value go up. He and Sue got the idea for the book last March, when their then-6-year-old daughter, Jamie, brought home her first Beanie Baby. After discovering there was no buying guide, they immediately set about writing one.

The Foxes will try anything. They lost $60,000 on their previous venture, a self-published novel about an alleged secret son of Elvis Presley. Total sales: 200 copies. Another book, *The Pizza and Ice Cream Diet*, sold 11 copies. Not surprisingly, no publisher would back their Beanie Baby idea.

So the Foxes published it themselves, using their daughter's $100,000 college fund. When book distributors shied away, the Foxes peddled it from home, and a mass mailing to 300 toy stores had a hit rate of nearly 50%. Demand surged. So did bookstore chain orders.

It's hard to get precise revenue figures for books; the *New York Times* refuses to disclose sales of a bestseller. The Foxes say the guide sold a million copies last year, and 1.1 million so far in 1998. Sounds wild, but Barnes & Noble reports up to 20,000 copies are flying off the shelves each week, faster than any other collectibles guide, ever.

The Foxes net $1 per book; each one retails for $6.95—pretty good margins in

Sue, Les and Jamie Fox
Next Beanie Baby: Tinker the Tulip?

publishing. With their pay dirt, they're building a new home. They're also designing more Beanie Baby projects, including a cookbook and trading cards; they've already made a CD.

Demand for Beanie Babies has begun to cool, according to toy stores around the country. No one can remember the last time frantic parents stormed a place rumored to be carrying a new shipment.

The Foxes are prepared for the worst. They've started sketching out a book on antique American birdhouses—they collect those, too. If that flops, it might make good company for all those unsold Elvis books.

It's not toy money

Toy line	Barbie	Beanie Babies	Hot Wheels	G.I. Joe	PEZ	G.I. Joe
Product	Ponytail Barbie #1	Peanut (dark blue elephant)	Volkswagen Beach Bomb	G.I. Nurse	Make-a-Face dispenser	Japanese Imperial Soldier
Year made	1959	1995	1969	1967	1972	1966
Maker	Mattel	Ty	Mattel	Hasbro	PEZ Candy	Hasbro
Estimated value	$10,000	$5,200	$4,000	$4,000	$3,200	$1,000

Beanie Babies can command prices higher than the rarest of toys.

Sources: Toy Shop magazine.

PHOTOGRAPHS © TO TO *THE WORLD OF BARBIE DOLLS BY PARIS AND SUSAN MANOS, THE BEANIE BABY HANDBOOK BY LES & SUE FOX, TOMART'S PRICE GUIDE TO HOT WHEELS COLLECTIBLES, HASBRO, INC.*
COLLECTING PEZ BY DAVID WELCH, ©1998 VINCLAT SANTELMORFAUSE PUBLICATIONS, THE OFFICIAL 30TH ANNIVERSARY SALUTE TO G.I. JOE

Forbes ▪ April 6, 1998

Great story...although we do not necessarily agree with all of the comments in this article, especially the last two paragraphs!

BEANIE BABIES
THE "UNOFFICIAL" STORY

The Beanie Baby phenomenon thrives on total chaos!

In our opinion, that's the philosophy of toymaker Ty Warner. And to some extent, it may be true. In the 1997 edition of The Beanie Baby Handbook we quoted Forbes' magazine's label of the unparalleled success of Beanie Babies as "Mystique Marketing." Mystique marketing, according to Forbes (who interviewed Les and Sue Fox in April, 1998 - see feature story on page 16) is the intentional creation of "empty shelves." By adding an aura of mystery to a product that would normally be available in unlimited supply, that product quickly disappears. It's never happened like this before. Ever!

From time to time, Beanie Babies are readily available. That is, you can walk into a toy store or gift shop and find a couple of dozen varieties of Beanies. The Ty company doesn't seem to mind this situation, as long as it's not constant. It makes Ty Warner just a little bit nervous when the public starts to think you can actually buy the Beanie Baby of your choice any time you want. For if that were the case, you could buy it tomorrow, or next month, rather than now. They'd rather keep you guessing. If you haven't noticed, Ty is into "surprises." (More about that in a minute.) The point is, Beanie Babies are different than any other toy in history. First, they're better. The "mysterious" success of Beanie Babies isn't really a puzzle at all. The darn things are incredibly cute, they're made surprisingly well, and the price is irresistible. Like they say, what's not to like?

We therefore continue to believe in the future of Beanie Babies. They will be around in 5 years, 10 years and beyond. They will continue to have "curb appeal" as well as collector appeal. Kids (and parents) will continue to like them and want them and cuddle them and play with them...and, most importantly, to buy them! End of story? Not quite. Back to our theory of chaos (which governs the entire universe), coupled with the element of surprise, and how this relates to the "Unofficial" vs. the "Official" Beanie Baby story.

The dictionary defines chaos as: "complete disorder and confusion." Are Beanie Babies "chaotic"? Not really. You just think they are, and that's what counts. In reality, nothing could be further from the Beanie Baby truth. In order to produce hundreds of millions, possibly billions, of Beanie Babies, Ty, Inc. must keep on top of a thousand marketing situations. They must buy miles of yards of fabric. (We'd love to publish photos, but they won't give us any.) They must follow strict manufacturing schedules. They must arrange complex national and international transportation. They must temporarily warehouse (in a 300,000 square foot building) sorted and unsorted Beanie Babies for distribution to 100,000 customers. They must send out a zillion detailed invoices. They must...well, you get the picture. (We wonder how many Beanie Baby eyeballs Ty keeps in stock?)

Many people have called Ty, Inc. "disorganized." The fact is, you can't run a business the size of Beanie Babies (not to mention the rest of Ty's fabulous line of plush toys) by being disorganized. The trick is to make it seem that way. Sure, there are glitches in production and distribution. That happens to everyone. But mostly (we think) it's planned. Planned chaos! Do you believe it's an accident that your neighborhood toy store never has all of the current issues? It's not. So even when a store offers a good selection of the little critters, some are "curiously" missing. Is Ty making fewer Prance the Cats? Are they about to flood the market with Erins? Who knows? Like Ty said when they announced their "Official" club: "Less is more." Those three words are probably the most telling statement Ty has ever made.

CHAOS AND TEDDY BEARS

In addition to a certain degree of chaos (which occasionally backfires), Ty loves surprises. After hyping their big forthcoming (supposedly) April 1, 1998 announcement of retirements and new releases, Ty decided to make this an "April Fool's Day" joke. Sorry, no releases or retirements until May 1. Then, a month later, only retirements, and a whopping 28 retirements at that! The rumor then began that new toys would be released on Mother's Day, including a special Mother's Day Teddy Bear. (We even published the rumored poem in our newsletter!) Did it happen? Nope. A week after Mother's Day, Ty announced that the wait would continue until May 30th. By the way, teddy bears are the backbone of Beanie Babies. Many of Ty's Teddy Bears are steeped in controversy (just the way he likes it!) We feel this will continue to happen. After all, teddies have been the world's most popular toy since 1902! We consider Beanie Babies a cross between Steiff Teddy Bears (which we still collect) and Barbie Dolls.

Ty meets Steiff

Some people say The Beanie Baby Handbook, and the McDonald's promotions, are two major reasons why public interest in Beanie Babies remains at a fever pitch. Interestingly, while the McDonald's event (see pages 42 & 67 for details) is "Officially" sanctioned by Ty, this book (and all of our other Beanie Baby activities) is not. Indeed, not only are we the most successful unauthorized, unaffiliated and unofficial collector's guide of all time...but as it turns out this is the best possible arrangement for us *and* Ty.

As you can see, the authors of this book are into fun. We like to guess how many Beanie Babies Ty made, as well as to try to predict the future. We've done a pretty good job so far, as our 1997 and 1998 editions attest to. By not merely being a spokesperson for Ty, while truly loving his toys, we come across as a breath of fresh, honest air. In other words, what you see is what you get! (Right or wrong.) Ty, on the other hand, can safely retain its role as the elusive phantom, neither confirming nor denying the myriad of rumors that claim to quantify and explain the phenomenon. Meanwhile, hundreds of millions of Beanies continue to roll off the conveyor belts and into the hearts of tens of millions of collectors.

Actually, we did try to convince Ty Warner to make us "official" back in 1997, but luckily he didn't take us up on our offer. Instead, Ty has either ignored our many requests for information and approval, or coyly suggested that he "sort of" likes what we are doing. (Or so we think.) The fact is, Ty has kept us guessing just the way he keeps you guessing about Beanie Babies. Based on this "cordial but unofficial" relationship, we'll keep guessing, and hopefully the Beanie Baby Beat will go on for years to come.

For those who wonder seriously about how we come up with our statistics, it isn't all guesswork. We do "unofficial" surveys among dealers and collectors to try to determine who's getting what. We calculate how many toys each of 100,000 stores gets monthly (100 toys per store = 10 million toys per month = 120 million toys per year.) And we use Sherlock Holmes logic to deduce certain theories. For example, the least popular toys will be discontinued, making them excellent investment candidates. But, of course, Ty sometimes discontinues the *most* popular toys, confounding even the most clever sleuth. In the end, it's still guesswork.

We like to think of our conclusions as "educated" guesswork. Will we look smart in 10 years? We hope so. But one of our favorite fortune cookie proverbs will always be: "The only thing we really know about the future is that it will surprise everyone."

Everything You Need To Know About...
BEANIE BABY TAGS

Beanie Baby tags may seem complicated, so let's simplify. First, other than for proper references, most collectors don't care about a Beanie Baby's "rear end" or "tush" tag...as long as it's intact! The most important tag on a Beanie Baby is the cardboard heart-shaped "Ty" tag, also known as a "hang" tag.

First Generation Tag (1993-1994)
The first generation hang tag is a single tag. It's also the only version in the shape of a full heart. This tag appeared on the original 9 and other early Beanie Babies. Most were detached and discarded, so these tags are collector's items.

Second Generation Tag (1994-1995)
The second generation hang tag is a double tag. Like its successors, the left part of the heart is missing. This tag is folded into a booklet of two attached hearts. On the right-hand heart is a "To / From" section for gift use.

Third Generation Tag (1995-1996)
The third generation hang tag is the same booklet format with fatter lettering. Inside is the same "To / From" set-up and, as before, the Style Number.

Fourth Generation Tag (1996-1997)
The fourth generation hang tag is the same as the third generation tag with 5 noteworthy changes: A poem, a birthday, a yellow star, no black outline on "Ty," and Ty's website address.

Fifth Generation Tag (1998-Current)
The newest Ty hang tag contains very subtle changes. The interior type style (& inside the star) is new, the birthday is spelled out and the Style # has been omitted.

In general, Beanie Babies without hang tags are worth only 50% to 75%, of their full value. Creased tags also depreciate the value of a toy. In the case of important rarities demand for mint condition examples sometimes minimizes the discount. Plastic tag protectors are the best way to prevent tag damage.

In response to the hundreds of questions people ask about tag errors, here's a good general answer. Only a tiny percentage of all Beanie Baby collectors care about tag errors. Mistagged Beanies are not especially valuable. A tush mis-tag is better than a hang mis-tag, but as a rule tag errors add only $10 to $25 to the value of a toy. On the other hand, rare and highly collectible tags (like "Brownie") are extremely valuable.

IMPORTANT: Beanies with "early" tags are worth $25 to $100 more.

ENTER
THE NATIONAL
BONGO & CONGO
Art Contest

(No Purchase Necessary)

DRAW OR PAINT YOUR PICTURE (IN COLOR) ON ANY 8½" X 11" SURFACE

Age Limit:
14 Years
Old

Contest
Deadline:
Nov. 1, 1998

RULES OF CONTEST: Simple! Just draw or paint a "detailed" picture of Bongo and Congo on paper, board or canvas. (All entries remain the property of West Highland Publishing.)

Your picture must be based on the lyrics to our popular Beanie Baby Song, "Bongo & Congo" (See next page for lyrics.) Show America's favorite baby gorilla and monkey acting out a scene from the song. Be sure to play the music while you're drawing for extra inspiration!

Artwork will be judged by a panel of foxy experts (Les, Sue and Jamie Fox) on the basis of originality and talent. Winners will be notified in November. Prizes sent Fed Ex. Top 3 winning pictures will be published (with artists' photos) in the 1999 Beanie Baby Handbook.

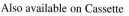

Send Your Entry (with name & address) To:
West Highland Publishing Co., Inc.
P.O. Box 36, Midland Park, NJ 07432

FIRST PRIZE	$1,000
SECOND PRIZE	500
THIRD PRIZE	250

Plus 50 Runner-Up Prizes!
A Matched Pair of Bongo & Congo Beanie Babies!

BONGO & CONGO

Written By Les & Sue Fox   © Copyright 1997

DEEP IN THE JUNGLE
(BOM-BOM-BAH-BOM-BOM)
A GORILLA NAMED CONGO
(BOM-BOM-BAH-BOM-BOM)
HAD A BEST FRIEND,
(DRUM SOUNDS CONTINUE)
A MONKEY NAMED BONGO.
BUT POOR BONGO
WAS ACCIDENT PRONE.
HOW DO YOU LIKE THAT?

IN THE SHADE OF A PALM TREE
(BOM-BOM-BAH-BOM-BOM)
THEY SHARED A BANANA
(DRUM SOUNDS CONTINUE)
TILL BONGO REACHED UP
AND A COCONUT FELL.
HIT CONGO IN THE HEAD
JUST LIKE A HAMMER.
HOW DO YOU LIKE THAT?

AND BONGO SAID:
"IT WAS AN ACCIDENT.
I DIDN'T MEAN TO DENT
YOUR GREAT BIG, HAIRY SKULL."
AND CONGO SAID:
"YOU BETTER BEAT IT, MAN!

RUN AS FAST AS YOU CAN.
AND DON'T COME BACK...FOR THE
REST OF YOUR NATURAL LIFE."

SO BONGO RAN AWAY
(BOM-BOM-BAH-BOM-BOM)
AND GATHERED HIS FRIENDS:
ROARY THE LION,
STRIPES THE TIGER,
SPIKE THE RHINO,
HAPPY THE HIPPO.
HOW DO YOU LIKE THAT?

AND THEY ALL CAME BACK
(BOM-BOM-BAH-BOM-BOM)
TO THE COCONUT TREE,
AND BONGO TOLD CONGO,
"MY FRIENDS WILL PROTECT ME!"
AND CONGO TOLD BONGO:
"I'M FEELING MUCH BETTER.
I GUESS I WAS
UNDER THE WEATHER,
THERE'S NO REASON TO FIGHT."
SO THE ANIMALS PLAYED CHECKERS,
RIGHT IN THE JUNGLE,
ALL THROUGH THE NIGHT! HOW DO
YOU LIKE THAT?

"Bongo & Congo" is one of 5 Original Beanie Baby Songs on Les & Sue Fox's music CD. Also includes: "Beanie Babies Are Here To Stay!", "Spot Without A Spot", "I Never Met a Beanie Baby I Didn't Like" and "Meet The Beanies."
(Complete Lyrics In The 1998 Beanie Baby Handbook)

America's Bestselling Beanie Baby Music
NOW AVAILABLE IN STORES!
Only $6.95
Also available on Cassette

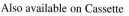
23

Meet "Clubby!"

Clubby is Ty's first "Limited Edition" Beanie Baby!

He was only available to members of Ty's "Official" Club. So we suggest you join today for future offers.

The complete story of Clubby and the Ty "Official" Club will appear in our 1999 edition.

Introducing...
The New
May, 1998 Releases

and
The New McDonald's
Teenie Beanie
Babies

The "New" Beanies
Introduction

Ty does it again! On the pages ahead you will find photos, current values and a collector's guide to buying the 14 "latest and greatest" Beanie Babies plus the 12 newest Teenie Beanies. This brings the total number of all varieties of Beanies to 210 (including Clubby.) That number breaks down to 188 regular size Beanie Babies and 22 McDonald's Teenies.

What can we say about the new May toys...except: "Wow!" As always, Ty has satisfied kids' and adults' desire for more exciting and different bean-stuffed animals to add to their growing collections. And at only $5 - $7 apiece (the McDonald's toys were free if you were hungry enough!), how can you lose? The answer is, you really can't. Beanie Babies, in our opinion, remain one of the best buys in America, and everyone knows it. In fact, if you got your McDonald's Beanies for free and if you pay an average of $6 for the new Ty releases, you'll spend a grand total of only $84.00 for 26 fantastic toys that could be worth well over $1,000 in 10 years! We'll even bet that at least one of these toys will be worth $100 within 2 years! (Guess which one. We're not telling.)

Don't forget. In order to have a chance to see your toys appreciate in value, you need to keep them in perfect mint condition. This means (if you can afford it), maybe you ought to buy two of each, one to play with and one to put away as a possible investment. Of course, no one really knows what the future will bring, but the worst you can do is wind up giving away the duplicates as birthday presents. Not a bad deal either. (NOTE: We recommend locket type "tag protectors" for all your Beanies. Plus, keep your collectable McDonald's toys in their sealed baggies. "M.I.P." (Mint In Package) Teenie Beanies are worth more than "loose" toys.)

By the way, don't be too quick to pay $10-$15 (or higher) for some of the new releases that may seem hard to get. It is the intention of Ty, Inc. to try to make all of these toys available to kids at approximately the $5 suggested retail price. It's our best guess that all 14 May releases will (at least for a few months) be available at the $5 - $7 price. At that level, you're bound to come up smelling like a rose by the first Spring of the new Millennium!

☼ ANTS ☼
(The Anteater)

Most anteaters love to eat bugs

Than eat an ant or harm a fly!

But this little fellow gives big hugs

He'd rather dine on apple pie

 Birthday: November 7, 1997

TOTAL BORN: 1,000,000   **Likely to be Retired: 2001**
Est. Survival (2008): 100,000

ISSUE PRICE	$5.00 - $7.00
1998 Value	$5.00 - $7.00
Year 2008 (est.)	$60.00

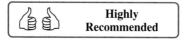 **Highly Recommended**

BEANIE HUNTER TIPS: As we predicted, Ty created a Beanie anteater...known in some circles as an aardvark. We still like our suggested name of "Bugs", but that's life. This is a great toy to play tug o' war with, as long as you don't bend the heart-shaped tag! Seriously, Ants is as cute as can be. If he acts politely (and agrees to vacuum your livingroom rug), it's okay to feed him a little sugar in the palm of your hand. (See Pages 203-204 of the regular 1998 edition.)

☼ EARLY ☼
(The Robin)

Early is a red breasted robin

NEW FOR '98

This happy robin loves to sing!

For a worm he'll soon be bobbin'

Always known as a sign of spring

🎂 **Birthday: March 20, 1997**

TOTAL BORN:	**1,000,000**	**Likely to be Retired: 2001**
Est. Survival (2008):	**100,000**	

ISSUE PRICE	**$5.00 - $7.00**
1998 Value	**$5.00 - $7.00**
Year 2008 (est.)	**$60.00**

👍👍 **Highly Recommended**

BEANIE HUNTER TIPS: You'll find "Early The Robin" listed as a "Future Beanie Baby" on Page 204 of the regular 1998 edition of The Beanie Baby Handbook. Better early than never! And how did we know that this adorable winged creature would soon fly off the drawing board? Simple. Our spies discovered thousands of tiny plush blue eggs all over Chicago!

FETCH
(The Golden Retriever)

Fetch is alert at the crack of dawn

NEW FOR '98

This little puppy is the one for you!

Walking through dew drops on the lawn

Always golden, loyal and true

Birthday: February 4, 1997

TOTAL BORN: 1,000,000   **Likely to be Retired:** 2001
Est. Survival (2008): 100,000

ISSUE PRICE	**$5.00 - $7.00**
1998 Value	**$5.00 - $7.00**
Year 2008 (est.)	**$60.00**

Highly Recommended

BEANIE HUNTER TIPS: Once again, another Fox "educated guess" turns into reality. "Blondie" the Golden Retriever was the name we suggested for this playful pooch. This very popular breed was the number one pick of our millions of readers for a new Beanie Baby, and that makes us very, very happy. "Fetch" is a clever name, too, and we're never disappointed with Ty's creativity. Just remember, Fetch is only a puppy. He's going to grow a lot bigger, so make room for him.

☼ FORTUNE ☼
(The Panda)

Nibbling on a bamboo tree

NEW FOR '98

Only a few are still around!

This little panda is hard to see

You're so lucky with this one you found

 Birthday: December 6, 1997

TOTAL BORN: 1,000,000 **Likely to be Retired: 2000**
Est. Survival (2008): 100,000

ISSUE PRICE	**$5.00 - $7.00**
1998 Value	**$5.00 - $7.00**
Year 2008 (est.)	**$100.00**

 **Highly Recommended**

 BEANIE HUNTER TIPS: Thank goodness for another wonderful Ty Panda Beanie! (Fortune is a real cookie!) With the price of Peking up in the stratosphere (and many fakes), Beanie collectors can heave a collective sigh of relief and quickly whip out a five-spot (and maybe a couple of singles.) If you're loaded, it's okay to track down a perfect Peking, too. But now everyone finally has a chance to own the world's most popular bamboo chomper. Next: A new camel?

30

GIGI
(The Poodle)

Prancing and dancing all down the street

NEW FOR '98

She's a dog that is anything but plain!

Thinking her hairdo is oh so neat

Always so careful in the wind and rain

Birthday: April 7, 1997

TOTAL BORN: 1,000,000   **Likely to be Retired: 2001**
Est. Survival (2008): 100,000

ISSUE PRICE	**$5.00 - $7.00**
1998 Value	**$5.00 - $7.00**
Year 2008 (est.)	**$60.00**

Highly Recommended

BEANIE HUNTER TIPS: And yet another Fox prediction comes true. We named our Poodle "Fluffy" but Gigi is equally appropriate. Bonjour, Gigi! Beefing up the canine line-up, Gigi will probably appeal more to girls than to boys as she's obviously la femme mystique. But don't worry, fellas. Fetch and Tracker will make you feel like a real He-Man!

31

GLORY
(The Bear)

Wearing the flag for all to see

New for '98

Happy Birthday USA!

Symbol of freedom for you and me

Red white and blue - Independence Day

Birthday: July 4, 1997

TOTAL BORN: 1,000,000 **Likely to be Retired:** 1999
Est. Survival (2008): 100,000

ISSUE PRICE $5.00 - $7.00
1998 Value $5.00 - $7.00
Year 2008 (est.) $150.00

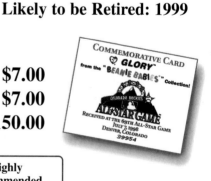

COMMEMORATIVE CARD
GLORY
from the "BEANIE BABIES" Collection!
COLORADO ROCKIES
ALL-STAR GAME
RECEIVED AT THE 69TH ALL-STAR GAME
JULY 7, 1998
DENVER, COLORADO
39954

Highly Recommended

BEANIE HUNTER TIPS: At first glance, we thought that Ty had created a Beanie Baby with star-shaped chicken pox! But Glory the Bear is simply very patriotic. From head to toe, he's an All-American teddy bear sporting the American Flag on his chest as proof positive. Actually, Glory originally had a green card...but we learned that he was just holding it for Erin, who recently recited the Pledge Of Allegiance and became an official U.S. citizen.

32

✿ JABBER ✿
(The Parrot)

Teaching Jabber to move his beak

NEW FOR '98

Teach him a new word every day!

A large vocabulary he now can speak

Jabber will repeat what you say

 Birthday: October 10, 1997

TOTAL BORN: 1,000,000 **Likely to be Retired: 2000**
Est. Survival (2008): 100,000

ISSUE PRICE	$5.00 - $7.00
1998 Value	$5.00 - $7.00
Year 2008 (est.)	$80.00

 **Highly Recommended**

BEANIE HUNTER TIPS: Our name for a Beanie Baby parrot was "Squawk" (see Page 204 of the regular '98 edition), but Jabber uses the same concept. Repeat after me: "I will proserve and pretect my pretty pet parrot. I will preserve and protect my pretty pet parrot. I will preserve and pretect my petty preet parrot..." (It's a tongue twister, silly!)

JAKE
(The Mallard Duck)

Jake the drake likes to splash in a puddle

NEW FOR '98

He's so glad you're here to play!

Take him home and give him a cuddle

Quack, Quack, Quack, he will say

 Birthday: April 16, 1997

TOTAL BORN: 1,000,000 **Likely to be Retired: 2001**
Est. Survival (2008): 100,000

ISSUE PRICE	**$5.00 - $7.00**
1998 Value	**$5.00 - $7.00**
Year 2008 (est.)	**$60.00**

Highly
Recommended

BEANIE HUNTER TIPS: Vaguely resembling "Duckie" the Tied-Died Duck invented by Carly and Zachary Hill of Nashville, Tennessee, Jake is a good mate for the recently retired Quackers. Actually, Jake was named for a young man who lives in Tampa, Florida, the grandson of Jerry Bauman, a cartoonist who sometimes hides Beanie Babies in trees for us.

 34

KUKU
(The Cockatoo)

This fancy bird loves to converse

You'll be surprised how he can rhyme!

He talks in poems, rhythms and verse

NEW FOR '98

So take him home and give him some time

Birthday: January 5, 1997

TOTAL BORN:	1,000,000	**Likely to be Retired: 2000**	
Est. Survival (2008):	100,000		

ISSUE PRICE	$5.00 - $7.00
1998 Value	$5.00 - $7.00
Year 2008 (est.)	$80.00

Highly
Recommended

BEANIE HUNTER TIPS: Kuku was a pleasant surprise, and is a fabulous addition to the beautiful Beanie Baby Birdie Brigade. As you probably know, the beak of a cockatoo is capable of biting a pair of handcuffs in two. So if you are ever locked up in a South American prison, and the nearest lawyer is drinking a Coors Light in Miami, whistle the theme song from "The High And The Mighty" and a "Kuku Bird" will fly to your rescue and snap open the steel bars of your window so you can jump on a horse and escape. (No kidding.)

35

✿ ROCKET ✿
(The Bluejay)

Rocket is the fastest bluejay ever

NEW FOR '98

He's so entertaining for you and me!

He flies in all sorts of weather

Aerial tricks are his specialty

 **Birthday: March 12, 1997**

TOTAL BORN:	1,000,000	**Likely to be Retired:**	2001
Est. Survival (2008):	100,000		

ISSUE PRICE	$5.00 - $7.00
1998 Value	$5.00 - $7.00
Year 2008 (est.)	$60.00

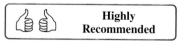 **Highly Recommended**

BEANIE HUNTER TIPS: Birds! Birds! Birds! What can we say except, "Chirp!" Once again, Ty has given us a delightful fair feathered friend to hold, to pet and to love. If you'd like this little fella to take a nap, hum him Elton John's classic "Rocket Man" but leave out the line, "In fact it's cold as — ." If your teacher says it's okay to bring Beanies to school, carry Rocket in your pocket while he's dozing.

 36

☼ STINGER ☼
(The Scorpion)

Stinger the scorpion will run and dart

Say hello and ask him to play!

But this little fellow is really all heart

NEW FOR '98

So if you see him don't run away

 Birthday: September 29, 1997

TOTAL BORN: 1,000,000 **Likely to be Retired: 1999**
Est. Survival (2008): 100,000

ISSUE PRICE	$5.00 - $7.00
1998 Value	$5.00 - $7.00
Year 2008 (est.)	$100.00

 **Highly Recommended**

BEANIE HUNTER TIPS: Bearing a remarkably similar physique to "Original 9" Beanie Baby "Pinchers", we predicted that Ty would produce a scorpion. No offense, oh omnipotent Beanie Baby makers, but our name ("Archie") was more original. (Arched tail = Archie? Get it, now?) No harm done. That is, as long as Stinger doesn't get a grip on you and let you have it with that venomous rear hypodermic!

☼ TRACKER ☼

(The Basset Hound)

Sniffing and tracking and following trails

NEW FOR '98

He's always happy when he's with you!

Tracker the basset always wags his tail

It doesn't matter what you do

 Birthday: June 5, 1997

TOTAL BORN: 1,000,000   **Likely to be Retired: 2001**
Est. Survival (2008): 100,000

ISSUE PRICE	**$5.00 - $7.00**
1998 Value	**$5.00 - $7.00**
Year 2008 (est.)	**$60.00**

 **Highly Recommended**

BEANIE HUNTER TIPS: Who can resist those "come hither" eyes...those elongated ears...or anything else about this welcome addition to the B.B.D.L.C.O.A. ("Beanie Baby Dog Lovers Club Of America.") Certainly not the authors of this book. So you'd better track down Tracker while his footprints are still fresh. (Did somebody say "McDonald's?") Hey, Ty guys, does this mean we're not going to get "Sniff" the Bloodhound?

 38

☼ WHISPER ☼
(The Deer)

She's very shy as you can see

NEW FOR '98

This little fawn will love you so much!

When she hides behind a tree

With big brown eyes and soft to touch

 Birthday: April 5, 1997

TOTAL BORN:	1,000,000	**Likely to be Retired: 2001**
Est. Survival (2008):	100,000	

ISSUE PRICE	$5.00 - $7.00
1998 Value	$5.00 - $7.00
Year 2008 (est.)	$60.00

 **Highly Recommended**

BEANIE HUNTER TIPS: This Bambi-like creature happily joins Ty's "Peaceable Kingdom" and waits patiently for someone to lead her to the tall, sweet grass. Shhh! Whisper has extremely sensitive ears. In fact, she's overheard many, many woodland secrets in her young life. Befriend and protect her and she might tell you who else is waiting on the other side of the Beanie Baby clearing.

WISE
(The Owl)

Wise is at the head of the class

NEW FOR '98

CLASS OF '98

Meet the newest graduate: Class of '98!

With A's and B's he'll always pass

He's got his diploma and feels really great

Birthday: May 31, 1997

TOTAL BORN: 1,000,000   **Likely to be Retired: 1998**
Est. Survival (2008): 100,000

ISSUE PRICE	$5.00 - $7.00
1998 Value	$5.00 - $7.00
Year 2008 (est.)	$125.00

👍👍 **Highly Recommended**

BEANIE HUNTER TIPS: Anybody around here (besides us) think that this big-brained bag of beans is the reincarnation of Hoot? As soon as Ty announced the release of "Wise," Professor Beanie knew that he had found his Beanie Baby soulmate. Wise has already signed a contract to help the professor with his "fairly difficult" questions for the 1999 Handbook. (Like: "What is Nip's real name?" Answer next year.)

ERIN
(The Bear)

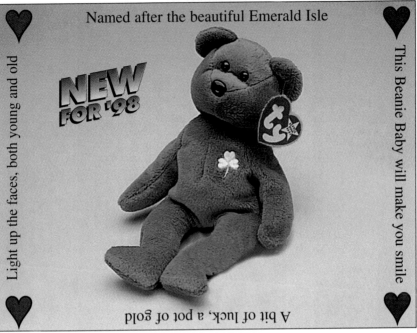

Named after the beautiful Emerald Isle

NEW FOR '98

Light up the faces, both young and old

This Beanie Baby will make you smile

A bit of luck, a pot of gold

Birthday: March 17, 1997

TOTAL BORN:	500,000	**Likely to be Retired: 1999**
Est. Survival (2008):	50,000	

ISSUE PRICE	**$5.00 - $7.00**
1998 Value	**$5.00 - $100.00**
Year 2008 (est.)	**$200.00**

Highly Recommended

BEANIE HUNTER TIPS: Erin is one of Ty's "current" but "currently hard to get" Beanie Babies. Like Britannia, Maple and Peace, Erin was originally issued in limited quantities. The supply of Erins is rumored to increase dramatically "soon." (Has it already happened?) Erin was actually released shortly after Valentine's Day, so we did not have time to include her in our last edition. So here she is! (The other bears are green with envy.)

Doby

McDonald's/Ty
Teenie Beanie Baby
#1

TOTAL BORN:	20,000,000	Birthday: May 22, 1998
Est. Survival (2008):	500,000	Retired: June 15, 1998

👍👍 Highly Recommended	ISSUE PRICE	$0.00 - $2.00
	1998 Value	$5.00 - $10.00
	Year 2008 (est.)	$60.00

Bongo

McDonald's/Ty
Teenie Beanie Baby
#2

TOTAL BORN:	20,000,000	Birthday: May 22, 1998
Est. Survival (2008):	500,000	Retired: June 15, 1998

👍👍 Highly Recommended	ISSUE PRICE	$0.00 - $2.00
	1998 Value	$5.00 - $10.00
	Year 2008 (est.)	$60.00

Twigs

McDonald's/Ty
**Teenie
Beanie Baby**
#**3**

TOTAL BORN:	20,000,000	Birthday: May 22, 1998
Est. Survival (2008):	500,000	Retired: June 15, 1998

Highly
Recommended

ISSUE PRICE	$0.00 - $2.00
1998 Value	$5.00 - $10.00
Year 2008 (est.)	$60.00

Inch

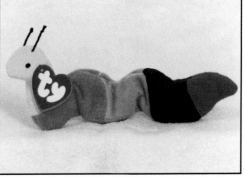

McDonald's/Ty
**Teenie
Beanie Baby**
#**4**

TOTAL BORN:	20,000,000	Birthday: May 22, 1998
Est. Survival (2008):	500,000	Retired: June 15, 1998

Highly
Recommended

ISSUE PRICE	$0.00 - $2.00
1998 Value	$5.00 - $10.00
Year 2008 (est.)	$60.00

Pinchers

McDonald's/Ty
**Teenie
Beanie Baby
#5**

TOTAL BORN: 20,000,000	Birthday: May 22, 1998
Est. Survival (2008): 500,000	Retired: June 15, 1998

Highly Recommended

ISSUE PRICE	$0.00 - $2.00
1998 Value	$5.00 - $10.00
Year 2008 (est.)	$60.00

Happy

McDonald's/Ty
**Teenie
Beanie Baby
#6**

TOTAL BORN: 20,000,000	Birthday: May 22, 1998
Est. Survival (2008): 500,000	Retired: June 15, 1998

Highly Recommended

ISSUE PRICE	$0.00 - $2.00
1998 Value	$5.00 - $10.00
Year 2008 (est.)	$60.00

Mel

McDonald's/Ty
**Teenie
Beanie Baby
#7**

| TOTAL BORN: | 20,000,000 | Birthday: May 22, 1998 |
| Est. Survival (2008): | 500,000 | Retired: June 15, 1998 |

Highly
Recommended

ISSUE PRICE	$0.00 - $2.00
1998 Value	$5.00 - $10.00
Year 2008 (est.)	$60.00

Scoop

McDonald's/Ty
**Teenie
Beanie Baby
#8**

| TOTAL BORN: | 20,000,000 | Birthday: May 22, 1998 |
| Est. Survival (2008): | 500,000 | Retired: June 15, 1998 |

Highly
Recommended

ISSUE PRICE	$0.00 - $2.00
1998 Value	$5.00 - $10.00
Year 2008 (est.)	$60.00

Bones

McDonald's/Ty
**Teenie
Beanie Baby
#9**

| TOTAL BORN: | 20,000,000 | Birthday: May 22, 1998 |
| Est. Survival (2008): | 500,000 | Retired: June 15, 1998 |

Highly
Recommended

ISSUE PRICE	$0.00 - $2.00
1998 Value	$5.00 - $10.00
Year 2008 (est.)	$60.00

Zip

McDonald's/Ty
**Teenie
Beanie Baby
#10**

| TOTAL BORN: | 20,000,000 | Birthday: May 22, 1998 |
| Est. Survival (2008): | 500,000 | Retired: June 15, 1998 |

Highly
Recommended

ISSUE PRICE	$0.00 - $2.00
1998 Value	$5.00 - $10.00
Year 2008 (est.)	$60.00

46

Waddle

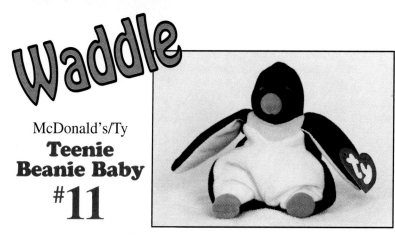

McDonald's/Ty
Teenie Beanie Baby
#11

TOTAL BORN:	20,000,000	Birthday: May 22, 1998
Est. Survival (2008):	500,000	Retired: June 15, 1998

Highly Recommended

ISSUE PRICE	$0.00 - $2.00
1998 Value	$5.00 - $10.00
Year 2008 (est.)	$60.00

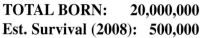

Peanut

McDonald's/Ty
Teenie Beanie Baby
#12

TOTAL BORN:	20,000,000	Birthday: May 22, 1998
Est. Survival (2008):	500,000	Retired: June 15, 1998

Highly Recommended

ISSUE PRICE	$0.00 - $2.00
1998 Value	$5.00 - $10.00
Year 2008 (est.)	$60.00

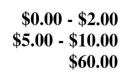

Beanie the
Pirate™

Kid Beanie™

Benny Beanie™

Beanie Bandito™

Professor Beanie™

Current & Retired Beanie Babies 1993-1998

The Complete Collection

Current & Retired Beanies
(1993-1998)
The Complete Collection

Including the 14 new Beanie Babies announced on May 30th, and McDonald's 12 new 1998 Teenie Beanie Babies (see "New Releases" section), there are now 209 different collectibles in the entire Ty Beanie Baby series. (Plus Clubby = 210!)

The "regular" edition of The Beanie Baby Handbook (issued on Valentine's Day) contains more detailed information about each Beanie Baby: Birthday, Total Born, Estimated 10-Year Survival Rates & Price Predictions, Likely To Be Retired, Beanie Hunter Tips, etc. This mid-year "Collector's Special Edition" contains complete details for only the May '98 releases. For the rest of the toys, we provide only a current value.

The exact current value of a Beanie Baby is hard to determine. Some people consider the highest price paid for a perfect Beanie with a perfect tag to be the "current" value. From this price deductions are made for a bent or creased hang tag (10% - 25%), a missing tag (25% - 50%) and minor imperfections like stains or tears. We disagree with reporting the highest price paid as an accurate representation of current value. In our opinion, "current value" should be considered the average price paid for a perfect toy. For example, collectors have shelled out as much as $5,000+ for a Royal Blue Peanut. But few serious collectors would generally agree to pay more than $3,500 to $4,000. In fact, with a little patience you can probably negotiate for a perfect "Royal Blue" at the $3,000 level. While we actually paid $3,500 for our Nana (see back cover) its true current value is $500 less. (NOTE: Other "experts" claim Nana is worth $4,500.) Prices of the rare Teddies are also "highly speculative." (Buy rare Beanies only from very reliable dealers.)

As a rule, if a Beanie Baby is not "near-mint" it has little collector's value. For example, Garcia the Bear is currently worth $150. (If you need one badly, expect to pay more like $200.) Without its hang tag, Garcia drops to $75. Put a nice little rip in the fabric, or lose and eye or nose button, and Garcia becomes just another bag of beans! On the other hand, true rarities like Tie-Dyed Lizzie can still command $300 in slightly worn condition! Bottom line: Don't play by the rules, because there aren't any! Beanie Babies are not Blue Chip stocks! They're a lot more fun, and sometimes more profitable, but prices "float" constantly. It takes guts and knowledge to make the best possible deal on rare Beanie Babies. And so, despite our 10-year price predictions, we do not recommend pulling your money out of the bank to invest in any kind of toys unless that is your personal choice.

Happy Beanie Hunting!

The Beanie Baby Collection

Ally the Alligator

Current Value: $40

Ants the Anteater

Current Value: $5-7

Baldy the Eagle

Current Value: $15-20

Batty the Bat

Current Value: $5-7

Bernie the St. Bernard

Current Value: $5-7

Bessie the Brown & White Cow

Current Value: $45

Blackie the Bear

Current Value: $5-7

Blizzard the White Tiger

Current Value: $25

Bones the Dog

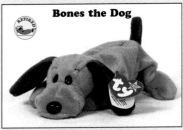

Current Value: $20

Bongo the Monkey

Dk. Tail $25-50, Lt. Tail $6, Nana $3000

The Beanie Baby Collection

Britannia the Bear

Current Value: $300-600

Bronty the Brontosaurus

Current Value: $800

Brownie the Bear

Current Value: $3,500

Bruno the Bull Terrier

Current Value: $5-7

Bubbles the Fish

Current Value: $100

Bucky the Beaver

Current Value: $20-40

Bumble the Bee

Current Value: $500

Caw the Crow

Current Value: $500

Chilly the Polar Bear

Current Value: $1,500

Chip the Calico Cat

Current Value: $5-7

The Beanie Baby Collection

Chocolate the Moose

Current Value: $5-7

Chops the Lamb

Current Value: $150

Claude the Tie-Dyed Crab

Current Value: $5-7

Congo the Gorilla

Current Value: $5-7

Coral the Tropical Fish

Current Value: $160

Crunch the Shark

Current Value: $5-7

Cubbie the Bear

Current Value: $15-30

Curly the Brown Bear

Current Value: $15-20

Daisy the Black & White Cow

Current Value: $5-7

Derby the Horse (Coarse Yarn)

Current Value: $12-15 (Spot $5-7)

The Beanie Baby Collection

Derby the Horse (Fine Yarn)

Current Value: $1,500-3,000

Digger the Crab

Current Value: Orange $600-700, Red $100-125

Doby the Doberman

Current Value: $5-7

Doodle/Strut the Rooster

Current Value: Doodle $40, Strut $10-15

Dotty the Dalmatian

Current Value: $5-7

Early the Robin

Current Value: $5-7

Ears the Bunny

Current Value: $10-15

Echo the Dolphin

Current Value: $10-15

Erin the Bear

Current Value: $5-100

Fetch the Golden Retreiver

Current Value: $5-7

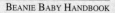

The Beanie Baby Collection

Flash the Dolphin

Current Value: $100-125

Fleece the Lamb

Current Value: $5-7

Flip the White Cat

Current Value: $25-35

Floppity the Lilac Bunny

Current Value: $15-20

Flutter the Butterfly

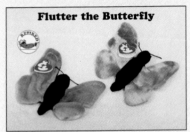

Current Value: $750

Fortune the Panda

Current Value: $5-7

Freckles the Leopard

Current Value: $5-7

Garcia the Tie-Dyed Teddy

Current Value: $160

Gigi the Poodle

Current Value: $5-7

Glory the Bear

Current Value: $5-7

The Beanie Baby Collection

Gobbles the Turkey

Current Value: $5-7

Goldie the Goldfish

Current Value: $30-40

Gracie the Swan

Current Value: $10-15

Grunt the Razorback

Current Value: $125-175

Happy the Grey Hippo

Current Value: $600

Happy the Lavender Hippo

Current Value: $15-20

Hippity the Mint Bunny

Current Value: $15-20

Hissy the Snake

Current Value: $5-7

Hoot the Owl

Current Value: $40

Hoppity the Rose Bunny

Current Value: $15-20

The Beanie Baby Collection

Humphrey the Camel

Current Value: $2,000

Iggy the Iguana

Current Value: $5-7

Inch the Inchworm (Felt)

Current Value: $125-175

Inch the Inchworm (Wool)

Current Value: $10

Inky the Tan Octopus

Current Value: $500

Inky the Pink Octopus

Current Value: $10-15

Jabber the Parrot

Current Value: $5-7

Jake the Mallard Duck

Current Value: $5-7

Jolly the Walrus

Current Value: $15-20

Kiwi the Toucan

Current Value: $175

The Beanie Baby Collection

Kuku the Cockatoo

Current Value: $5-7

Lefty the Democratic Donkey

Current Value: $275

Legs the Frog

Current Value: $15-25

Libearty the USA Bear

Current Value: $300

Lizzy the Tie-Dyed Lizzard

Current Value: $750-1,000

Lizzy the Blue Lizzard

Current Value: $15-25

Lucky the Ladybug

Current Value: 7 $125-150, 11 $15, 21 $400

Magic the Dragon

Current Value: $35

Manny the Manatee

Current Value: $100-150

Maple the Canadian Bear

Current Value: $200, Olympic $400, Pride $450

The Beanie Baby Collection

Mel the Koala

Current Value: $5-7

Mystic the Unicorn

Current Value: Tan $15-25, Striped $5-7

Mystic the Unicorn (Fine Yarn)

Current Value: $150-200

Nanook the Husky

Current Value: $5-7

Nip the Gold Cat

Large $350-550, All Gold $1,000, White Paws $15-25

Nuts the Squirrel

Current Value: $5-7

Patti the Maroon Platypus

Current Value: $500-750

Patti the Purple Platypus

Current Value: $10-15

Peace the Tie-Dyed Bear

Current Value: $35-50

Peanut the Royal Blue Elephant

Current Value: $3,500

The Beanie Baby Collection

Peanut the Light Blue Elephant

Current Value: $10-15

Peking the Panda

Current Value: $1,500

Pinchers the Lobster

Current Value: $10-15, Punchers $3,000

Pinky the Flamingo

Current Value: $5-7

Pouch the Kangaroo

Current Value: $5-7

Pounce the Brown Cat

Current Value: $5-7

Prance the Tabby Cat

Current Value: $5-7

Princess the Bear

Current Value: $5-100

Puffer the Puffin

Current Value: $5-7

Pugsley the Pug

Current Value: $5-7

The Beanie Baby Collection

Quacker the Duck (No Wings)

Current Value: $2,500

Quackers the Duck

Current Value: $10-15

Radar the Bat

Current Value: $200-250

Rainbow the Chameleon

Current Value: Tongue $5-7, No Tongue $15

Rex the Tyrannosaurus

Current Value: $750

Righty the Republican Elephant

Current Value: $275

Ringo the Raccoon

Current Value: $5-7

Roary the Lion

Current Value: $5-7

Rocket the Bluejay

Current Value: $5-7

Rover the Red Dog

Current Value: $15-25

The Beanie Baby Collection

Scoop the Pelican

Current Value: $5-7

Scottie the Black Terrier

Current Value: $10

Seamore the Seal

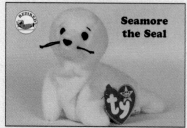

Current Value: $75-150

Seaweed the Otter

Current Value: $5-7

Slither the Snake

Current Value: $2,000-2,500

Sly the Fox (White Belly)

Current Value: $5-7

Sly the Fox (Brown Belly)

Current Value: $200-250

Smoochy the Frog

Current Value: $5-7

Snip the Siamese Cat

Current Value: $5-7

Snort the Bull

Current Value: $5-7

The Beanie Baby Collection

Snowball the Snowman

Current Value: $25-50

Sparky the Dalmatian

Current Value: $100

Speedy the Turtle

Current Value: $20-30

Spike the Rhinoceros

Current Value: $5-7

Spinner the Spider

Current Value: $5-7

Splash the Orca Whale

Current Value: $100-125

Spooky the Ghost

Current Value: $25-50

Spot the Dog

Current Value: No Spot $2,500, Spot $35-45

Spunky the Cocker Spaniel

Current Value: $5-7

Squealer the Pig

Current Value: $20-30

The Beanie Baby Collection

Steg the Stegosaurus

Current Value: $650-800

Sting the Manta Ray

Current Value: $150

Stinger the Scorpion

Current Value: $5-7

Stinky the Skunk

Current Value: $5-7

Stretch the Ostrich

Current Value: $5-7

Stripes the Dark Tiger

Current Value: $300 (Fuzzy Belly $500)

Stripes the Light Tiger

Current Value: $15-20

Tabasco the Bull

Current Value: $200-250

Tank the Armadillo

7 & 9 Plates $150-200, 9 Plates (small) $40-60

1997 Teddy

Current Value: $35-45

The Beanie Baby Collection

Teddy (Brown)

Current Value: Old $2,000-2,500, New $60

Teddy (Cranberry)

Current Value: Old $1,500, New $1,400

Teddy (Jade)

Current Value: Old $1,300, New $1,600

Teddy (Magenta)

Current Value: Old $1,200, New $1,400

Teddy (Teal)

Current Value: Old $1,300, New $1,600

Teddy (Violet)

Current Value: Old $1,300, New $1,700

Tracker the Basset Hound

Current Value: $5-7

Trap the Mouse

Current Value: $1,000

Tuffy the Terrier

Current Value: $5-7

Tusk the Walrus

Current Value: $135

The Beanie Baby Collection

**Twigs
the
Giraffe**

Current Value: $15-20

**Valentino
the Bear**

Current Value: $15-30

Velvet the Panther

Current Value: $15-25

Waddle the Penguin

Current Value: $10-15

Waves the Whale

Current Value: $10-15

Web the Spider

Current Value: $1,000

Weenie the Dachshund

Current Value: $15-20

Whisper the Deer

Current Value: $5-7

Wise the Owl

Current Value: $5-7

Wrinkles the Bulldog

Current Value: $5-7

The Beanie Baby Collection

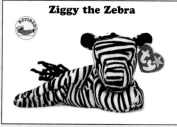

Ziggy the Zebra

Current Value: $10-15

Zip the Black Cat

Large $500-600, All Black $2,500, White Paws $45

In 1998, McDonald's issued a wide variety of Teenie Beanie "accessories" such as these beautifully enameled lapel pins for employees. Highly collectible! (Current Value of set: $200.00)

The 1999 Handbook will feature other Teenie Beanie items including a giant rooftop banner!

See next page for
1997 McDonald's Teenie Beanie Babies. ☞

The 1997 Teenie Beanie Baby Collection

Chocolate

Current Value: $25

Chops

Current Value: $30

Goldie

Current Value: $20

Lizz

Current Value: $15

Patti

Current Value: $25

Pinky

Current Value: $35

Quacks

Current Value: $15

Seamore

Current Value: $25

Snort

Current Value: $15

Speedy

Current Value: $20

68

Beanie Recipes

Food For Thought

As any truly incurable Beanieholic would ask, one day we asked ourselves: "Ourselves...What do Beanie Babies eat to maintain such soft, healthy-looking fur?" We figured there must be special foods, peculiar to each species, that keep all of our Beanie friends in such good shape and spirits.

To our delight we were able to communicate with most of the Beanies, through a translator of course. Except for a few close-mouthed Beanies (involuntarily sewn shut), we discovered 52 taste-tempting, nutritional treats the Beanie Babies consider their personal favorites. Now, let's make something perfectly clear. We do not promise that if you eat the same thing as Chip or Bones, you will soon have the same luxurious coat. Nor do we suggest that you will liver forever, as Beanies do.

However, we do promise that kids and moms and dads can have lots of fun preparing the "simple and easy" recipes. Of course, you must promise that you will share these recipes with your friends, relatives, schoolmates and any Beanie Baby collector who comes to visit. (We said *Beanie* collector, *not* tax collector!) You must also give us your word that if you take any really great pictures of yourself (or other victims) concocting our food ideas, you will mail them to us...no matter how sloppy anyone looks! We will publish the ones we like best in the 1999 edition of The Beanie Baby Handbook. (Photos will not be returned.)

By the way, despite her extraordinary culinary talents, "Beanie Chef" Jeanette Long (*pronounced "short"*) is not a French chef flown in from Paris. She's a former advertising executive, the mother of a beautiful eight year-old daughter (Aly) and a devoted Beanie Baby collector who just happens to live right around the corner from us. (Aly is one of our daughter Jamie's best friends.) Jeanette is a fantastic cook (and mom) who can whip up a delectable baloney sandwich, or anything in this book, at a moment's notice. All of the foods shown in the recipe section were created and prepared by our Beanie Chef. Jeanette worked closely with Beanie food critics Nip and Zip to perfect these original recipes. We (and the "Ip" Cats) hope you will find the time to make all of our 1998 recipes for meals, snacks, birthday parties and other important occasions. *Bon appetit!*

The Menu

Breakfast Treats
Top O' The Beanie Mornin' To You

Bumble And Blackie's Honey Granola - 78

Flip's One-Flip Pancakes - 80

Humphrey's Lumpy Oatmeal - 82

Stretch's Eggs In-A-Hole - 84

Tasty Snacks And Appetizers
Quick 'N Easy Savory Bites

Derby's Galloping Trail Mix - 86

Hissy's Breadstick Twists - 88

Quackers' Crackers - 90

Squealer's Pigs In Blankets - 92

Tabasco And Snort's Easy Nachos - 94

Waddle's Cream Cheese Penguins - 96

Sandwiches
Alternatives To The Golden Arches

Crunch's Crunchy Tuna Salad Sandwiches - 98

Inch's Foot Long Hero - 100

Lucky's Mini Pizzas - 102

Maple's Canadian BLT's - 104

Princess' Tea Sandwiches - 106

Trap's Grilled Cheese
Sandwiches - 108

Veggies, Salads & Side Dishes
Healthy And Delicious Fill-Me-Ups

Peking's Fried Rice - 112

Puffer's Puffy Potatoes - 114

Smoochy's Broccoli With
Cheese Sauce - 116

Twigs' Treetop Salad - 118

Entrees (Main Meals)
An Array Of International Flavorites

Chilly's Beary Good Chili - 120

Inky's Chicken Fingers - 122

Mel, Patti & Pouch's Shrimp On The Bar-B - 124

Slither's Slippery Spaghetti And Meatballs - 126

Yankee "Doodle's" Macaroni & Cheese - 128

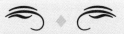

Breads And Muffins
Bake Up A Storm In The Afternoon

Caw's Corny Corn Bread - 130

Erin's Irish Soda Bread Muffins - 132

Cranberry Teddy's Cranberry Muffins - 134

Cookies
Tempting Tummy Pleasers

Ally's "Snappy" Ginger Cookies - 136

Bones' Painted Sugar Cookies - 138

Chip's Chocolate Chip Cookie Cups - 140

Mystic's Fresh Fruit Pizza Cookie - 142

Peanut's Peanutty Cookies - 144

Royal Peanut's Elegant Elephant Ears - 146

Valentino's Linzer Tarts - 148

Ziggy And Blizzard's Black & White Cookies - 150

(Princess' Tea Cookies, See Sandwiches - 106)

Delectable Desserts
Not For Calorie Counters!

Brownie's Famous Brownies - 154

Beanie Bunnies' Favorite Carrot Cake - 156

Chocolate's Chocolate "Moose" - 158

Kiwi's Tropical Shortcake - 160

Rex's Rocky Road - 162

Speedy's Caramel Pecan "Turtles" - 164

Spinner And Web's Creepy-Crawler Cupcakes - 166

Teenie Beanies' Teenie Weenie Cheesecakes - 168

Ice Cream Delights
Scoop Du Jour

Libearty, Lefty & Righty's Political Pie - 170

Pinky's Flamingo Flambé - 172

Seamore's Arctic S'Mores - 174

Snowball's Snowballs - 176

Fruits And Drinks
A Cornucopia Of Quenchers

Bongo & Congo's Chocolate Bananas - 178

Coral's Tropical Dessert Drink - 180

Daisy's Black Cow Float - 182

Rainbow's Fruit Kabobs - 184

Breakfast Treats

Tasty Snacks & Appetizers

Sandwiches

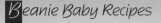
BUMBLE & BLACKIE'S HONEY GRANOLA

16 Servings

INGREDIENTS

3/4	cup honey
1/2	cup butter or margarine
1	teaspoon ground cinnamon
1	teaspoon vanilla
	dash salt
4	cups old-fashioned oatmeal
2	cups coarsely chopped nuts
1	cup raisins

A FOOD TIP FROM NIP & ZIP

"Two Claws Up!" raved Nip, after tasting just a tiny bite of this wonderful honey granola. Zip agreed, adding: "The only thing I don't like is the tiny portion size." Of course, since cats do a lot of exercise, Zip decided to eat Chip, Flip and Snip's portions as well as his own.

HOW TO MAKE 'EM

♥ Preheat oven to 350°.

♥ In a large mixing bowl, combine oats, nuts and raisins, mix well and put aside.

♥ In a small saucepan, combine honey, butter, cinnamon, vanilla and salt; bring to a boil and cook one minute.

♥ Pour honey mixture over the oat mixture and mix until well blended.

♥ Lightly grease a cookie sheet by rubbing about 1/2 of a teaspoon of butter over the entire pan.

♥ Spread the mixture on the baking sheet, and bake at 350° for about 15-20 minutes or until lightly browned (stir every 5 minutes). Let the mixture cool in the pan.

♥ Crumble and store in an air-tight container up to 2 weeks.

Benny Beanie's™ Nutritional Facts (per serving - 1/2 cup):
Calories 325; Fat 16g (Saturated 5g); Cholesterol 16mg;
Sodium 82mg; Carbohydrate 39g; Protein 7g

"Hey, Blackie!" said Bumble. "I hear a loud grumble.
"Perhaps it is time to indulge."
"Dear Bumble," said Blackie. "I think you are wacky.
"My stomach has not lost its bulge!"

Blackie the Bear

Bumble the Bee

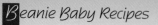

FLIP'S ONE-FLIP PANCAKES

2 Servings

INGREDIENTS

- 3/4 cup milk (can add up to 1 cup)
- 1 egg
- 2 tablespoon butter, melted
- 1 cup flour
- 2 teaspoons baking powder
- 2 tablespoons sugar
- 1/2 teaspoon salt

  maple syrup; jam; raspberries, blueberries or chopped apple; chocolate chips; nuts

A FOOD TIP FROM NIP & ZIP

Add blueberries, strawberries or chocolate chips. Top with whipped cream, maple and chocolate syrup. Delicately slice off one small, perfect triangle and freeze the rest! From Zip: Someone's been eating too much catnip!

HOW TO MAKE 'EM

♥ In a medium-sized bowl, add milk (start with 3/4 cup and add more, depending on how thick you like them.)

♥ Melt butter either in a microwave, or on top of the stove, and add to the bowl. Mix lightly.

♥ Break egg in a small bowl, then add to the milk mixture.

♥ In another bowl, add flour, baking powder, sugar and salt, mix well. Now add these 2 mixtures together.

♥ Beat mixture lightly with a spoon, do not over mix or this will toughen the pancakes. It is ok if the batter appears lumpy.

♥ Lightly grease a skillet or griddle with butter and heat over medium heat.

♥ Spoon batter onto skillet, into large or small pancakes. (Add chopped nuts, chocolate, or fruit if desired.)

♥ When bubbles start to appear and burst, flip pancakes.

♥ Cook other side of pancakes until lightly browned.

♥ Serve immediately with butter and syrup, or jam and fresh fruits.

♥ Serves four people "purrrfectly."

Benny Beanie's™ Nutritional Facts (per serving):
Calories 252; Fat 9g (Saturated 5g); Cholesterol 75mg;
Sodium 560mg; Carbohydrate 36g; Protein 6g

Grease up the griddle, get fit as a fiddle,
Pancakes are good for your diet.
Like Flip's friend Pounce, you won't gain an ounce
Unless of course you eat 'em...What a riot!

 Flip the Cat

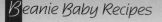
HUMPHREY'S LUMPY OATMEAL

2 Servings

INGREDIENTS

1-3/4 cups water
1 cup old fashioned oats
1/8 teaspoon salt, (optional)

butter or margarine
brown sugar
applesauce
chopped nuts
cinnamon
jam or jelly
vanilla ice cream

A FOOD TIP FROM NIP & ZIP

Before embarking on a trip from say, Cairo to Jerusalem, Humphrey recommends consuming approximately 24 gallons of oatmeal plus 48 gallons of water. A proportionately smaller amount will get you through recess and gym in school.

HOW TO MAKE 'EM

♥ Put water in small saucepan, add salt and heat on high heat until boiling.

♥ Stir in oats and cook 4-5 minutes over medium heat; stirring occasionally.

♥ Pour cereal into bowl, and add your favorite topping

Tasty Toppings for Humphrey's Lumpy Oatmeal:

♥ <u>Butter or margarine and brown sugar:</u> Put 1 teaspoon of butter on your oatmeal. Top with 1 tablespoon brown sugar. Stir.

♥ <u>Apple and cinnamon:</u> Add 1 tablespoon of cool applesauce and lightly sprinkle with cinnamon.

♥ <u>Jam or jelly:</u> Add your favorite jam or jelly and stir.

♥ <u>Ice cream cool off:</u> Scoop a tablespoon of vanilla ice cream over hot oatmeal. Tastes great and cools off your cereal quickly.

Benny Beanie's*™ *Nutritional Facts (per serving):
Calories 157; Fat 3g (Saturated 0g); Cholesterol 0mg;
Sodium 7mg; Carbohydrate 27g; Protein 6g

> Kids love oatmeal, kids love lumps.
> Kids look like camels when they have the mumps.
> Breakfast is the best way to start your day,
> Ask Mom and Dad. See what they say!

 Humphrey the Camel

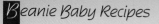

STRETCH'S EGG IN-A-HOLE

1 Serving

INGREDIENTS

- 1 slice bread, thickly sliced if possible
- 1-2 teaspoons butter
- 1 egg
- salt and pepper

A FOOD TIP FROM NIP & ZIP

As our resident food critics, both Nip and Zip were consulted by the Beanie Chef before this particular recipe was finalized. Nip's suggestion is to pour ketchup all over your egg. Zip feels that this dish is best served "without" much garnish. What do you think?

HOW TO MAKE 'EM

♥ Cut from an unsliced loaf of bread, 1 1" thick slice; or 1 pre sliced piece of bread. Cut out a circle from the center using a small round cookie cutter, or drinking glass with a 2" to 2-1/2" rim.

♥ Melt 1 teaspoon of butter in a skillet over medium heat. When it sizzles, add the bread along with the cut out circle. Cook about 1 minute, until lightly browned.

♥ Flip the bread and the cut out over using a large pancake turner. Add more butter if pan becomes dry.

♥ Break egg into a cup, and pour into the hole in the bread. Sprinkle egg with salt and pepper. Cover skillet with lid. Cook 3-4 minutes until egg is cooked through.

♥ Serve with cut out on the side.

Benny Beanie's™ Nutritional Facts (per serving):
Calories 178; Fat 10g (Saturated 4g); Cholesterol 224mg;
Sodium 247mg; Carbohydrate 14g; Protein 9g

Have you heard about an ostrich's brain?
It's the size of a pea. What a pain.
But Stretch has the answer, it's eating cooked eggs
It expands his mind right into his legs.

Stretch
the Ostrich

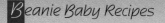

DERBY'S GALLOPING TRAIL MIX

8 Servings

INGREDIENTS

1/2 cup candy coated chocolate pieces

1/2 cup raisins

1 cup peanuts

2 cups round toasted oat cereal, or puffed corn cereal

HOW TO MAKE 'EM

♥ In a medium sized plastic bag, place candy coated chocolate pieces, raisins, peanuts and cereal. Close bag tightly and shake to mix.

♥ Store mix in a plastic bag, or container, in a cool place – up to 3 weeks.

♥ Great for taking on long trips or hikes. You may also add additional ingredients such as gummy candies, or pretzels.

A FOOD TIP FROM NIP & ZIP

Needless to say, you should not be riding your horse (or your bike or skateboard) while eating a snack. However, Nip often tosses back a few mouthfuls of Derby's Mix just before he takes his afternoon cat nap. Both he and Zip find that this combination of foodstuffs is an all-natural sleep inducer.

Benny Beanie's™ Nutritional Facts (per serving - 1/2 cup):
Calories 215; Fat 13g (Saturated 3g); Cholesterol 5mg;
Sodium 89mg; Carbohydrate 21g; Protein 6g

Whoa! Big horsie! You're making me nauseous
When I eat and ride, I'm usually cautious.
Slow down, big fella, and save your lungs,
Slow down before we bite our tongues!

Derby the Horse (Fine Mane)

Derby the Horse (Coarse Mane)

Derby the Horse (with spot)

HISSY'S BREADSTICK TWISTS

8 Servings

INGREDIENTS

2	tablespoons olive oil
2	tablespoons grated Parmesan cheese
1-1/2	tablespoons poppy seeds
1-1/2	tablespoons sesame seeds
2	cloves garlic, crushed, or minced
1	11oz. package refrigerated breadstick dough
8	raisins, cut in 1/2

A FOOD TIP FROM NIP & ZIP

Be sure to brush your teeth after eating Hissy's Breadstick Twists. Unless you're a snake, it's not very attractive to walk around with a white blob stuck between your two front teeth. Nip and Zip also recommend a little mouthwash to get rid of that powerful garlic breath.

HOW TO MAKE 'EM

♥ Preheat oven to 375°.

♥ In a small bowl, mix olive oil, grated cheese, poppy seeds and sesame seeds.

♥ Crush garlic with a press, or finely chop, and add to seed mixture.

♥ Separate dough into 8 breadsticks, and stretch each one into 2 foot long pieces.

♥ Place breadsticks on baking sheets, twisting and curling into snake-like shapes.

♥ Spread seed mixture onto each breadstick, using a spoon and clean fingers!

♥ Add 2 raisin halves to one end for the eyes and 1 red pepper strip for the tongue.

♥ Bake about 10-14 minutes, or until golden.

Benny Beanie's™ Nutritional Facts (per serving - 1 stick):
Calories 125; Fat 2g (Saturated 1g); Cholesterol 0mg;
Sodium 290mg; Carbohydrate 19g; Protein 3g

Strong and hungry, Hissy's on the move
Headed for the kitchen, he's in a groove.
When Hissy eats a breadstick, he can really rock 'n' roll
See the shape of his body? He swallowed it whole!

Hissy the Snake

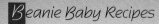
QUACKERS' CRACKERS

INGREDIENTS

CRACKERS: Wheat, sesame, saltines, rye wafers, cheese crackers

ASSORTED CHEESES: Cheddar, Muenster, Provolone, Swiss, Mozzarella, Cream cheese

TOPPINGS: Olives, bacon bits, cherry tomato slices, red pepper strips, pineapple chunks, apple and pear slices, peanut butter, roast beef, turkey, ham

HOW TO MAKE 'EM

♥ Place assorted crackers on a serving plate.

♥ Top each cracker with toppings of your choice, or use some of the following suggestions:

- Sliced Ham and Swiss.
- Sliced Roast beef and Muenster.
- Mozzarella and tomato and black olive slices.
- Sliced Turkey, cheddar and bacon bits.
- Peanut butter and bacon bits.
- Peanut butter and apple slices.
- Cheddar cheese and apple slices.
- Muenster and pear slices.
- Sliced ham and pineapple.

♥ Decorate each cracker with cheese cut outs, olive slices, parsley, green onion or red pepper strips.

♥ Be creative and enjoy!

A FOOD TIP FROM NIP & ZIP

Many people (and even some pussy cats) overlook the true potential of crackers as a main dish as well as an appetizer. Thinly sliced filet mignon or Lobster Thermidor are just two toppings that may be enhanced by the careful application above or between Quackers' Crackers.

Benny Beanie's™ Nutritional Facts (per serving - 4 crackers):
Calories 160; Fat 12g (Saturated 4g); Cholesterol 24mg;
Sodium 370mg; Carbohydrate 12g; Protein 9g

Salt or no salt, wingless or wings,
Quackers loves crackers (among other things).
In soup or on salads, as a snack in the woods
Crumbled-up crackers taste awful good!

Quackers the Duck

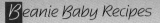

SQUEALER'S PIGS IN BLANKETS

8 Servings

INGREDIENTS

- 2 8 oz. packages refrigerated crescent rolls
- 1 16 oz. package cocktail frankfurters
- 1/2 cup mustard, (optional)
- 1/2 cup ketchup, (optional)

HOW TO MAKE 'EM

♥ Preheat oven to 375°F.

♥ Unroll dough, separating into 4 pieces, keep 2 crescents together by wetting each seam and pinching together. This leaves you with 4 rectangles per package.

♥ Roll out 1 rectangle at a time on lightly floured board to a thickness of about 1/8".

♥ Cut each rectangle into 6 strips about 3" long.

♥ Roll frankfurter in strips, seal ends with cold water. Arrange seam side down, 2" apart on ungreased baking sheet.

♥ Bake 10-12 minutes until golden.

♥ Serve hot, with mustard or ketchup.

♥ Makes about 48 pigs in blankets. Serves 8 as appetizers.

A FOOD TIP FROM NIP & ZIP

Try dipping these petite treats in a light and fragrant dijon mustard sauce, inhale deeply to enjoy. (Careful when you breathe in! Practice the Heimlich Maneuver.) P.S.: Frozen cocktail franks can be micro-waved to near-perfection in 60 seconds.

Benny Beanie's™ Nutritional Facts (per serving - 6 pieces): *Calories 390; Fat 27g (Saturated 2g); Cholesterol 35mg; Sodium 1070mg; Carbohydrate 42g; Protein 9g*

When she's not squirming around in her muddy sty,
Squealer the pig is baking a pie.
Everyone who tastes her wares says thanks,
And takes home a piggie bag of cocktail franks.

Squealer
the Pig

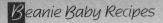

TABASCO AND SNORT'S EASY NACHOS

6 Servings

INGREDIENTS

1	16 oz. can refried beans, heated
4	cups packaged tortilla chips
1-1/2	cups cheddar cheese, shredded
1/4	cup jalapenos, sliced

salsa
sour cream, (optional)
guacamole, (optional)
sliced olive, (optional)
chopped green onion, (optional)

HOW TO MAKE 'EM

♥ SPREAD beans onto the bottom of a large oven proof serving dish.

♥ Arrange chips over beans.

♥ Top with cheese and jalapenos.

♥ PLACE under preheated broiler, 4 inches from the heat, for 1-2 minutes or until cheese is melted. Or place in microwave oven for about 1 to 1-1/2 minutes.

♥ Top with salsa, sour cream and any or all additional toppings.

A FOOD TIP FROM NIP & ZIP

Your gourmet pals, Nip and Zip, heartily urge you to pile all four optional add-ons atop your Nachos. They further suggest that you take little bitty bites, carefully balancing these delectable appetizers so they don't land on your shoe. No sharing, please!

Benny Beanie's™ Nutritional Facts (per serving):
Calories 381; Fat 19g (Saturated 6g); Cholesterol 30mg; Sodium 838mg; Carbohydrate 38g; Protein 13g

Originally from South of the Border,
Nachos have become a popular order.
They may taint your breath, but you won't feel full
Unless you attempt to devour the bull!

Tobasco the Bull

Snort the Bull

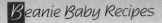

WADDLE'S CREAM CHEESE PENGUINS

18 Servings

INGREDIENTS

5-3/4   ounce can jumbo black olives, pitted, (about 18)

1   8 oz. package cream cheese

18   small black olives, pitted

18   toothpicks, frilly ones if possible

1   carrot, at least 6 inches long and 1 inch in diameter

HOW TO MAKE 'EM

A FOOD TIP FROM NIP & ZIP

Deep-frozen cream cheese penguins may be used to play checkers or chess outdoors during the winter. Bring along plenty of extras in a Zip-Loc bag. You'll probably work up quite an appetite, especially if you forget to put on your long underwear.

♥ Cut a slit from top to bottom, lengthwise, into each jumbo olive, one side only. Carefully insert about 1 teaspoon of cream cheese into each olive.

♥ Cut the carrot into 18 1/4 inch slices. Cut a small notch out of each carrot slice to form feet. Save the cut out piece and press into center of small olive to form the beak. (If necessary cut a small slit into each olive before inserting the beak.)

♥ Using a frilly toothpick, if possible, stack head, (small olive), body (big olive – large hole side down, facing feet) and feet (carrot slice), adjusting so that the beak, cream cheese chest and notch in the carrot slice line up.

♥ You can add scarves and hats by using fresh red pepper strips, or canned pimentos cut into different shapes.

♥ Makes 18 Waddles appetizers.

Benny Beanie's™ Nutritional Facts (per serving - 1 penguin): Calories 47; Fat 4g (Saturated 3g); Cholesterol 14mg; Sodium 39mg; Carbohydrate 1g; Protein 1g

Wrap one cute penguin in iceberg lettuce
Let us see where that will get us.
Do penguins come from the top of the earth?
Taste one and see, for what it's worth.

Waddle the Penguin

CRUNCH'S CRUNCHY TUNA SALAD SANDWICHES

2 Servings

INGREDIENTS

1	6 oz. can Tuna fish, drained
1	tablespoon mayonnaise
1	stalk celery, chopped
4	slices bread, any type
1	tablespoon pickle relish (optional)

HOW TO MAKE 'EM

♥ Open can of tuna fish, drain off as much water or oil as possible.

♥ In a small bowl, add drained tuna, and using a fork, break into flakes.

♥ Wash, and chop celery stalk, and add to bowl.

♥ Add mayonnaise and relish and stir well with a fork.

♥ Spread tuna mixture evenly on 2 slices of bread.

♥ Now place the other 2 slices on top.

♥ Cut sandwiches into quarters, and serve with pickles or potato chips to make even crunchier!

♥ Makes 2 crunchy sandwiches.

A FOOD TIP FROM NIP & ZIP

If you're watching your weight, tuna is a healthy and filling meal. ("Hold the extra mayo!") In addition to the ingredients listed in this simple recipe, you can spice up your non-fattening tuna sandwich with sliced tomato and, if you dare, a thin slice of Vidalia onion when in season.

Benny Beanie's™ Nutritional Facts (per serving - 1 sandwich):
Calories 278; Fat 8g (Saturated 2g); Cholesterol 4mg;
Sodium 725mg; Carbohydrate 44g; Protein 8g

Do you remember that movie, "Jaws"?
It's got nothing to do with Beanies because
Crunch isn't a Great White killer shark,
He just likes to eat tuna salad in the park.

Crunch the Shark

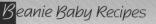
INCH'S
FOOT LONG HERO

12 Servings

INGREDIENTS

1	large loaf Italian bread
2	ounces Swiss cheese, sliced
2	ounces turkey breast, sliced
2	ounces salami, sliced
2	ounces ham, sliced
2	ounces provolone cheese, sliced
1	whole tomato, sliced
1	cup lettuce, shredded
	Italian salad dressing (optional)

A FOOD TIP FROM NIP & ZIP

This "Italian Hero" may look the same as that $1.99 special at your local convenience store, but if you make it fresh it sure won't taste the same. Unfortunately, the home-made version can't be used as a football or doorstop either.

HOW TO MAKE 'EM

♥ Slice bread in half, lengthwise.

♥ Layer the Swiss cheese, turkey, salami, ham and provolone cheese.

♥ Top with lettuce and tomato slices, drizzle Italian dressing over all.

♥ Cut into 12, 1-inch pieces. Hold together with toothpicks.

♥ Serve with olives, potato chips, and carrot curls.

♥ Serves 12 1-inch slices.

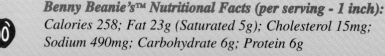
Benny Beanie's™ Nutritional Facts (per serving - 1 inch):
Calories 258; Fat 23g (Saturated 5g); Cholesterol 15mg;
Sodium 490mg; Carbohydrate 6g; Protein 6g

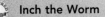

Inch hates to put his foot in his mouth
Especially since he has no feet
He's sure you won't be heading south
Once you bite into his tasty treat!

Inch the Worm

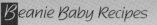

LUCKY'S MINI PIZZAS

6 Servings

INGREDIENTS

6	whole English muffins, halved
2	cups tomato sauce
2	cups grated mozzarella cheese
1	cup medium black olives, sliced in half widthwise
6	colossal black olives, halved, lengthwise
1/2	cup grated Parmesan cheese

HOW TO MAKE 'EM

♥ Preheat broiler. Cut muffins in half, and arrange on a cookie sheet.

♥ Spread 1 tablespoon of sauce on each muffin half.

♥ Sprinkle with 2 tablespoons mozzarella and a sprinkling of Parmesan.

♥ Cover the cheese with another tablespoon of sauce.

♥ Arrange 1 large olive half at one end to form head. Place 4 or 5 olive halves, round side, up to form dots.

♥ Slide tray into the broiler. Broil until cheese is melted and sauce is hot.

♥ Remove from oven. Let cool so you don't burn your mouth.

A FOOD TIP FROM NIP & ZIP

If you've never tasted ladybug style pizza before... "Try it...you'll like it!" As you can see, this dish gets its name from its resemblance to the ripe, tomato-red back of America's most beloved insect. But it still gets its flavor from Old Italy!

Benny Beanie's™ Nutritional Facts (per serving - 2 halves):
Calories 351; Fat 16g (Saturated 7g); Cholesterol 36mg;
Sodium 1471mg; Carbohydrate 35g; Protein 17g

Pick your Lucky number and toss the dice
(If it's your wedding, toss the rice!)
This dish serves six, plus six more cousins
Just double the recipe, it's cheaper by the dozen!

 Lucky the Ladybug

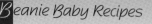

MAPLE'S CANADIAN BLT'S

2 Servings

INGREDIENTS

- 4 slices Canadian-style bacon
- 4 slices bread, any type, or English muffin
  lettuce
- 1 tomato
  butter or mayonnaise

HOW TO MAKE 'EM

♥ In a small frying pan, heat 4 slices of Canadian bacon. Set aside.

♥ Toast bread, and spread lightly with butter or mayonnaise.

♥ Place lettuce on 2 slices of bread, and top with a slice of tomato.

♥ Top each sandwich with 2 slices of Canadian bacon, and the remaining slices of bread.

♥ Cut in half and serve with pickles, olives or carrot curls.

♥ Makes 2 sandwiches.

A FOOD TIP FROM NIP & ZIP

In Nip's humble opinion, the Beanie Chef's Canadian BLT will prove to be the number one crowd pleaser. Zip isn't so sure. He finds this admittedly delicious temptation "one of the best recipes in the book" but refuses to rank it above number three. Merits your immediate attention!

Benny Beanie's™ Nutritional Facts (per serving - 1 sandwich): Calories 216; Fat 4g (Saturated 1g); Cholesterol 19mg; Sodium 766mg; Carbohydrate 32g; Protein 13g

While skiing through Ontario
Maple was eating Cheerios,
He needed a little TLC
So he ordered a Canadian BLT!

GONE HUNTING

Maple the Bear

PRINCESS' TEA SANDWICHES

4 Servings

INGREDIENTS

assorted breads, thinly
   sliced
butter, softened, or
   mayonnaise
cream cheese, softened
ham, thinly sliced
roast beef, thinly sliced
peanut butter
jam

tuna fish salad,
   (see Crunch's Tuna
   sandwich filling)
lettuce
tomato
egg salad, recipe below
cucumber, peeled and
   thinly sliced

A FOOD TIP FROM NIP & ZIP

These mouth-watering mini-feasts contain only a few calories apiece, yet deliver the "oomph" of sandwiches twice as fattening. Following in the royal tradition (cats were considered gods in ancient Egypt), the rhyming cats of The Beanie Baby Handbook wear a 20-pound gold and diamond crown while consuming this modern delicacy.

HOW TO MAKE 'EM

- ♥ If desired, spread each slice of bread with a very light coating of butter or mayonnaise.
- ♥ Choose any, or all of the fillings below, or make up your own filling.
- ♥ Top each buttered slice of bread with a small amount of filling, and, if desired, some lettuce, cucumber, or tomato.
- ♥ top with another slice of bread.
- ♥ Cut off the crusts, and cut each sandwich into quarters, triangles and or slices.
- ♥ Sandwiches can also be cut out with cookie cutters.
- ♥ Garnish with parsley, or whatever looks attractive and tasty.

Suggested Fillings: • tomato and sliced cheese • tuna salad • peanut butter and jelly or jam • egg salad (combine finely chopped boiled eggs with mayonnaise and a tiny bit of mustard and pickle relish) • Ham and cheese • Roast beef and cream cheese

PRINCESS' TEA COOKIES

8 Servings

INGREDIENTS

1/2	cup butter
1/3	cup sugar
1	egg yolk only
1	teaspoon vanilla extract
1	heaping cup flour
1/2	cup powdered sugar

- ♥ Preheat oven to 350° – In a medium sized mixing bowl, cream together the butter and sugar. This can be done by hand or with electric mixer.
- ♥ Add to the bowl the egg yolk.
- ♥ Add the vanilla and the flour, and mix thoroughly.
- ♥ Shape into tiny balls about 1 teaspoon each, and place onto ungreased baking sheets.
- ♥ Press slight indents into the center of each ball, either using your finger or a thimble. Fill each hole with a tiny bit of jam.
- ♥ Bake for 12-15 minutes, until the edges are slightly golden. Remove from oven and cool completely.
- ♥ Roll edges in powdered sugar. Makes about 45 cookies.

Benny Beanie's™ *Nutritional Facts (tea sandwiches - approx., depends on filling).*
Calories 50; Fat 4g (Saturated 2g); Cholesterol 5mg; Sodium 104mg; Carbohydrate 4g; Protein 3g
Benny Beanie's™ *Nutritional Facts (tea cookies - 4 per serving):*
Calories 154; Fat 8g (Saturated 5g); Cholesterol 38mg; Sodium 79mg; Carbohydrate 19g; Protein 1g

Princess' Tea Sandwiches are fit for a king,
Imagine the joy that four can bring
On a grey afternoon when it's drizzling outside
And your soul needs someplace cozy to hide.

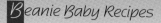

TRAP'S GRILLED CHEESE SANDWICHES

2 Servings

INGREDIENTS

- 4 slices bread, any kind
  butter
- 4 slices American cheese, or any of your favorite cheeses
  mustard, (optional)
  tomato slice, (optional)
- 1/4 apple, thinly sliced, (optional)

HOW TO MAKE 'EM

- ♥ Take two slices of bread, spread with mustard, if you like.
- ♥ Top these two pieces of bread with American cheese, or enough cheese of any kind to cover. (If you'd like, at this time add either a slice or two of tomato, or apple slices.)
- ♥ Top with remaining bread.
- ♥ Place frying pan on medium heat. Add small amount of butter to cover bottom of the pan, just enough so sandwiches will not stick!
- ♥ Place sandwiches in frying pan.
- ♥ Grill on one side until golden. Turn with spatula and cook on other side. Cut each sandwich in half.

A FOOD TIP FROM NIP & ZIP

Trap the Mouse was interviewed by Zip while sampling the very first cheese sandwich to slide off the Beanie Chef's grill. His mouth was full, but his mumbled evaluation was clear: "Good enough for Mickey himself!"

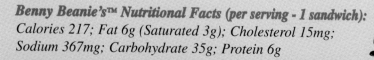

Benny Beanie's™ Nutritional Facts (per serving - 1 sandwich):
Calories 217; Fat 6g (Saturated 3g); Cholesterol 15mg;
Sodium 367mg; Carbohydrate 35g; Protein 6g

Squeaky, squeaky, squeaky clean,
Trap the Mouse is on the scene.
Eating grilled cheese and making a bet
To exit before the trap is set.

Trap the Mouse

Veggies, Salads & Side Dishes

Entrees (Main Meals)

Breads & Muffins

Cookies

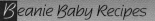
PEKING'S FRIED RICE

6 Servings

INGREDIENTS

- 2 tablespoons vegetable oil
- 1 teaspoon salt
- 1 onion, diced fine
- 1 stalk celery, diced fine
- 2 eggs, beaten
- 1 cup frozen peas and carrots
- 1 cup bean sprouts, fresh or canned
- 6 cups cold cooked rice
- 3 tablespoons soy sauce, or to taste
- 2 scallions, diced, green part only

A FOOD TIP FROM NIP & ZIP

Both Nip and Zip agree wholeheartedly with Peking that fried rice is a delicacy to be savored without worrying about etiquette. The cats also recommend playing with a ball of moist fried rice before digging in!

HOW TO MAKE 'EM

♥ Heat oil in a large non stick frying pan.

♥ Add salt to the pan, then add onion and stir until tender.

♥ Add celery and stir until it begins to change color.

♥ Stir in eggs, keep stirring until the eggs begin to cook through.

♥ Add frozen peas and carrots, cover pan with a lid, and continue to cook 5 minutes, over low heat.

♥ Remove the lid and add rice, stir until rice is heated through and separated.

♥ Stir in soy sauce and cook until rice is a nice light brown color.

♥ Stir in scallions and serve hot.

Benny Beanie's™ Nutritional Facts (per serving - 1-1/4 cups): *Calories 391; Fat 7g (Saturated 1g); Cholesterol 71mg; Sodium 1056mg; Carbohydrate 72g; Protein 10g*

On a visit to the Orient,
Peking sat next to the President
He took the chopsticks and said, "Very nice.
But I use my paws to eat fried rice!"

Peking the Panda

PUFFER'S PUFFY POTATOES

4 Servings

INGREDIENTS

- 2 large baking potatoes
- 1/2 stick butter
- 1/2 cup milk
- 1/2 teaspoon salt
- 1/4 teaspoon pepper
- 1-1/2 cups cheddar cheese, grated
- 3 tablespoons Parmesan cheese

A FOOD TIP FROM NIP & ZIP

Nip rates this tasty potato treat as a great entree as well as a side dish. Zip says you'll enjoy these almost as much as a large fries at McDonald's.

HOW TO MAKE 'EM

♥ Under running water, wash the skin of the potatoes. Dry well, and prick several holes in each potato with a fork. (This is to prevent the potato from exploding in the oven.)

♥ Bake potatoes in an oven or microwave. In regular oven, preheat to 425°, and bake for 1 hour. In a microwave, bake on high for 10 minutes. When time is up, pierce with a fork to make sure the potato is done, (fork should go in easily).

♥ Cut each cooked potato in half, lengthwise. Scoop out the insides of the potato with a spoon.

♥ Place the potato insides into a mixing bowl, and add butter. Mash with a fork or potato masher.

♥ Add milk and whip with an electric mixer, until fluffy.

♥ Add salt and pepper and 1/2 of the grated cheddar and mix well.

♥ Spoon potato mixture back into the skins, and top with the rest of the cheddar and Parmesan. Bake until the cheese melts. You can put the potato under the broiler to brown the top lightly, if desired.

Benny Beanie's™ Nutritional Facts (per serving - 1/2 potato):
Calories 336; Fat 18g (Saturated 11g); Cholesterol 56mg;
Sodium 675mg; Carbohydrate 28g; Protein 16g

If the potato famine hits again
(And who's to say just where or when?)
There'll still be plenty for the puffins,
They've frozen a million potato muffins!

Puffer the Puffin

SMOOCHY'S BROCCOLI WITH CHEESE SAUCE

4 Servings

INGREDIENTS

1	head broccoli, trimmed of leaves and lower stalk
1/3	cup milk
1-1/2	cups cheddar cheese, or sliced processed cheese

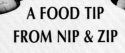

A FOOD TIP FROM NIP & ZIP

It may be impolite to "nip" off the broccoli florets, but that's how Nip likes to eat this veggie dish. Zip usually gets stuck with the stalks, but since they're dripping with oodles of cheddar cheese, he rarely complains.

HOW TO MAKE 'EM

♥ Place broccoli on a cutting board and remove all large leaves, and most of the stalk. Cut broccoli into florets, leaving only a small amount of the stalk.

♥ Put broccoli into a large bowl, and wash well.

♥ In a 9" or 10" skillet put about 1" of boiling water, add broccoli and cook, covered for about 10 minutes. This can also be done in a large pot with a steamer basket.

♥ Once the broccoli has cooked to the desired tenderness, drain well in a colander over the sink.

♥ Place broccoli into a serving dish.

TO MAKE THE CHEESE SAUCE

♥ In the top part of a double boiler, set over simmering water, add milk and cheese of your choice.

♥ Heat, stirring constantly, until blended and smooth.

♥ Remove from heat, and pour over cooked broccoli.

Benny Beanie's™ Nutritional Facts (per serving - 1 cup):
Calories 224; Fat 15g (Saturated 9g); Cholesterol 47mg;
Sodium 304mg; Carbohydrate 7g; Protein 15g

The cheese may be a little sticky
But it melts like butter and tastes sublime
Smoochy hops right to the table
When his mother calls: "It's broccoli time!"

Smoochy the Frog

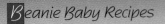
TWIGS'
TREETOP SALAD

4 Servings

INGREDIENTS

1	head lettuce, washed and torn
1	pint cherry tomatoes
6	radishes, washed and sliced
1	stalk celery, chopped
1	cup carrots, grated
1/2	cup cheddar cheese, grated
1	whole cucumber, peeled and sliced
1/2	cup almonds, slivered

A FOOD TIP FROM NIP & ZIP

Salad may be good for you, but Nip thinks you should add a little diced tuna and chicken to perk it up. Zip says the most important factor in enjoying Twigs' specialty is to use a salad fork and bowl with your name on it.

HOW TO MAKE 'EM

♥ Use a knife to remove the core from head of lettuce.

♥ Hold lettuce under cold running water, cut side up, so that water goes into the lettuce. Wash thoroughly, and drain, cut side down.

♥ Tear lettuce leaves into bite sized pieces, and put them into a bowl.

♥ Prepare other ingredients by cleaning, peeling, slicing and /or chopping.

♥ Add ingredients to the salad and mix.

♥ Add your favorite dressing, or use the simple Italian dressing below.

DRESSING

6	tablespoons olive oil
2	tablespoons red wine, or balsamic vinegar
1/8	teaspoon powdered mustard
1/8	teaspoon sugar
	salt and pepper to taste

Mix all together in a small bowl, stir until well blended. Serve over salad.

Benny Beanie's™ Nutritional Facts (per serving):
Calories 257; Fat 15g (Saturated 4g); Cholesterol 15mg;
Sodium 309mg; Carbohydrate 21g; Protein 10g

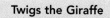

A "head" of lettuce, dressing on "top"
Keeps Twigs quite busy, he can't stop
Chewing and chomping and chowing down
Then he's up all night doing the town!

Twigs the Giraffe

CHILLY'S BEARY GOOD CHILI

4 Servings

INGREDIENTS

1	tablespoon butter
1	pound lean ground beef
1/2	cup onions, coarsely chopped
2-1/2	cups red kidney beans, drained
1/4	teaspoon garlic powder
1	10 3/4 ounce can condensed tomato soup
1	teaspoon salt
2	teaspoons chili powder

A FOOD TIP FROM NIP & ZIP

Zip always keeps an adequate supply of Tums "For Your Tummy" on hand when he eats chili. As Nip will testify to, it's not that the dish is so spicy. It's rather that Zip doesn't know when to stop. Zip denies this whole story, claiming he only picks at his chili. (Do you believe him?)

HOW TO MAKE 'EM

♥ Melt butter in a large skillet.

♥ Stir in ground beef and chopped onion.

♥ Cook the meat and onion mixture until both are well cooked, and lightly browned.

♥ Stir in garlic powder, drained kidney beans, can of tomato soup (do not add water!), salt, and 2 teaspoons of chili powder (more if you like it spicy!)

♥ Heat these ingredients just until they begin to boil.

♥ Reduce heat to low, and simmer for about 20 minutes, stirring several times.

♥ Serve chili in bowls, with rice, noodles, crackers, toast or Caw's Corny Corn bread.

Benny Beanie's™ Nutritional Facts (per serving):
Calories 367; Fat 20g (Saturated 8g); Cholesterol 87mg;
Sodium 1027mg; Carbohydrate 18g; Protein 28g

Never underestimate the power of beans,
Remember that food may not be what it seems.
Those innocent kidneys will make you feel silly
They heat up your insides, that's why it's called Chili!

 Chilly the Polar Bear

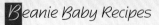

INKY'S
CHICKEN FINGERS

4 Servings

INGREDIENTS

- 1 egg
- 1/2 cup milk
- 1 teaspoon Dijon mustard
- 1/4 teaspoon salt
- 1/8 teaspoon black pepper
- 1/2 cup flour
- 1-1/2 cups corn flake crumbs
- 1-1/2 pounds boneless chicken breasts, cut into 1-1/2 x 1" pieces
- 1-1/2 tablespoons butter, melted

A FOOD TIP FROM NIP & ZIP

A "hand-y" way to fix a quick and healthy din-din! (Meow!) Like many of our Beanie Baby recipes, Inky's leftover chicken fingers may be wrapped and frozen for easy reheating in the microwave. (Breakfast?)

HOW TO MAKE 'EM

♥ Preheat oven to 350°.

♥ In a small bowl, stir together the egg, milk, mustard, salt and pepper. Whisk in the flour.

♥ Put corn flakes in a shallow plate. Dip chicken pieces in the egg mixture, then into the cornflakes, coat completely.

♥ Place chicken fingers onto an ungreased cookie sheet.

♥ Lightly brush chicken with melted butter.

♥ Bake in the oven for 20 minutes or until the chicken is cooked through and the outside is crispy.

♥ Serve with honey mustard sauce.

HONEY MUSTARD SAUCE

- 1/4 cup honey
- 1/4 cup Dijon mustard
- 1/4 cup mayonnaise

♥ In a small bowl, mix the honey, mustard and mayonnaise. Serve in a hollowed out red pepper for extra fun.

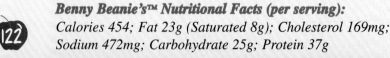

Benny Beanie's™ Nutritional Facts (per serving):
Calories 454; Fat 23g (Saturated 8g); Cholesterol 169mg;
Sodium 472mg; Carbohydrate 25g; Protein 37g

Inky the Octopus

MEL, PATTI & POUCH'S SHRIMP ON THE BAR-B

2 Servings

INGREDIENTS

- 1/2 pound large shrimp
- 3 tablespoons olive oil
- 2 tablespoons fresh lemon juice
- 1 clove garlic, crushed, or chopped
- 4 wooden skewers

A FOOD TIP FROM NIP & ZIP

Please be extremely careful when barbecuing. Seriously. That grill is very, very hot. If you touch it, your fingertips may become part of the menu. (Yukko!)

HOW TO MAKE 'EM

♥ Peel and wash shrimp in cold water. With the help of an adult, de-vein the shrimp. (See explanation in this book for this technique.)

♥ Peel the clove of garlic, and chop into tiny pieces using a small knife, or a garlic crusher.

♥ Place the oil and crushed garlic and lemon juice in a small bowl, add uncooked peeled and cleaned shrimp. Cover bowl with plastic wrap or foil, and marinate in refrigerator for at least 1 hour. At the same time, soak the skewers in a pan filled with water. This prevents the wood from drying out and burning while the shrimp are being cooked.

♥ After the shrimp has marinated for 1 hour, place about 4 shrimps on each skewer, and barbeque for 4 minutes on each side. Cook long enough so the shrimp starts to turn light brown. This can also be done indoors in an oven set on broil. Cooking time is about the same. Do not overcook or the shrimp will become tough.

♥ Serve with rice, or potato, and vegetables to make a meal.

Benny Beanie's™ Nutritional Facts (per serving):
Calories 323; Fat 24g (Saturated 3g); Cholesterol 222mg;
Sodium 255mg; Carbohydrate 2g; Protein 24g

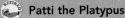

While traveling "down under"
Mel and Patti brought back for you
This fine Australian wonder
Straight from the kangaroo!

Mel the Koala

Pouch the Kangaroo

Patti the Platypus

SLITHER'S SLIPPERY SPAGHETTI & MEATBALLS

8 Servings

INGREDIENTS

MEATBALLS:

1	pound lean ground beef
2	eggs, lightly beaten
1	clove garlic, crushed
4	tablespoons grated Parmesan cheese
1/2	cup seasoned bread crumbs
1	tablespoon chopped parsley
	salt and pepper to taste
2	tablespoons olive oil

TOMATO SAUCE:

1	clove garlic, crushed
3/4	cup chopped onions
1	28 oz. can whole Italian plum tomatoes
1	28 oz. can crushed Italian plum tomatoes
1-1/2	cups water
1/4	cup fresh or 1 teaspoon dried basil
2	tablespoons olive oil
1/2	teaspoon salt
1/4	teaspoon pepper
1/2	teaspoon sugar
1/2	lbs. pasta of your choice

A FOOD TIP FROM NIP & ZIP

While it was cooking, Nip and Zip curled themselves around the Beanie Chef's ankles, begging for a taste of Slither's favorite pasta. They were rewarded with one big, fat meatball apiece which, unlike Slither, they did not swallow whole.

Meatballs:

- ♥ To make meatballs, put the ground beef in a large mixing bowl, add eggs, crushed garlic, Parmesan cheese, breadcrumbs, parsley, salt and pepper.
- ♥ Using your hands, mix the ground beef mixture until it is well combined, but do not over mix as this will toughen the meatballs.
- ♥ Divide ground beef mixture in half, divide each half into 12 even portions (this will make 24 small meat balls.) Shape each portion of ground beef into a meatball. Place meatballs on a plate.
- ♥ Heat oil in a frying pan on the stove over medium heat. Put meatballs in the pan and cook for about 10 minutes, turning occasionally with a wooden spoon to brown all sides. While the meatballs are browning, prepare tomato sauce.

Tomato sauce:

- ♥ Chop garlic and onion and set aside.
- ♥ Open cans of tomatoes and pour the entire contents into a large mixing bowl. Using your fingers, break up the tomatoes into small pieces.
- ♥ In a large 5 quart saucepot heat olive oil on the stove over medium heat. Add garlic and onions and cook until softened.
- ♥ Add tomatoes with the liquid, the water, the basil, the salt and pepper, and sugar. Stir mixture with a wooden spoon.
- ♥ Bring the sauce to a boil over high heat. Turn down the heat to low. Add the meatballs to the sauce and simmer for 1 hour.
- ♥ While the sauce is cooking, prepare spaghetti as the package instructions direct, using a 6 quart saucepot. When the spaghetti is done, turn off the heat, and with the help of an adult, drain in a colander in the sink. Keep the pasta warm until ready to serve.
- ♥ To serve, spoon some spaghetti into each serving bowl. Ladle some sauce and 3 meatballs on to each serving. Add Parmesan cheese and serve.

Benny Beanie's™ Nutritional Facts (per serving):
Calories 256; Fat 19g (Saturated 7g); Cholesterol 95mg; Sodium 300mg; Carbohydrate 7g; Protein 15g

Snake it around the prongs of your fork!
Eat it in Venice, or in New York!
Enjoy spaghetti all over the place,
Hey! What's that red stuff all over your face?

Slither the Snake

YANKEE "DOODLE'S" MACARONI & CHEESE

4 Servings

INGREDIENTS

- 8 cups water, boiling
- 1 teaspoon salt
- 1-1/2 cups elbow macaroni
- 1/2 pound sharp cheddar cheese, grated
- 2 tablespoons butter
- 4 teaspoons flour
- 1 cup milk
- salt and pepper

A FOOD TIP FROM NIP & ZIP

It was Zip's suggestion to "taste test" this popular food on 3,654 kids ages 6 to 12. Instead, Nip ate it all and gave it his top rating: "More!"

HOW TO MAKE 'EM

♥ Preheat oven to 350°.

♥ Put a large pot on the stove, add water, and 1 teaspoon of salt, and let the water come to a boil.

♥ Grate cheddar cheese into a bowl, and set aside.

♥ Once the water has boiled, slowly add macaroni, and stir with a long handled spoon. Stir 2 or 3 times the first few minutes to make sure the macaroni does not stick to the pot. Cook about 12 minutes, until tender. Drain the macaroni. Set aside.

♥ While the pasta is cooling, put 2 tablespoons of butter in a small saucepan and turn the heat to medium, melt the butter, taking care not to let it burn.

♥ With the flame still on add flour and mix together. Keep stirring the mixture about 2 minutes, until it is well blended, bubbly, and thickened.

♥ With the heat still on, add milk. Stir vigorously. When the sauce has thickened a little, and is smooth, turn off the heat.

♥ Add 1/2 of the cheese to the pan, and stir until cheese is melted. Taste, add a pinch of salt if needed.

♥ Pour macaroni into a 1-1/2 to 2 quart (6 to 8 cups) ovenproof baking dish.

♥ Pour the cheese sauce over the macaroni, and stir, until all noodles are well coated. Sprinkle the remaining 1/2 cup of cheese all over the top.

♥ Put the dish, uncovered, into the oven. Bake for 30-40 minutes.

Benny Beanie's™ Nutritional Facts (per serving):
Calories 474; Fat 27g (Saturated 17g); Cholesterol 83mg;
Sodium 517mg; Carbohydrate 35g; Protein 22g

Meet the rooster who rules the farm,
His name is Doodle and he loves cheese.
His favorite pasta is loaded with charm
If you like it, slap your knees!

Doodle the Rooster

CAW'S CORNY CORN BREAD

12 Servings

INGREDIENTS

1	cup yellow cornmeal
1	cup flour
1/4	cup sugar
1	tablespoon baking powder
1	teaspoon salt
2	eggs
1	12 oz. can corn, drained
1-1/4	cups milk
1/4	cup vegetable oil

A FOOD TIP FROM NIP & ZIP

Nip's family is originally from Kentucky, where corn bread is a family tradition. His grandfather swears that this recipe was stolen from a well guarded secret recipe kept in the governor's mansion. It's that good! (Zip is from Wisconsin. This is his first taste of corn bread and he loves it.)

HOW TO MAKE 'EM

♥ Preheat oven to 425°.

♥ Grease an 8x8x2 inch baking pan with butter.

♥ In a large mixing bowl add the cornmeal, flour, sugar, baking powder, and salt. Mix well.

♥ In a small bowl beat eggs with a fork. Add drained corn, milk and oil. Stir with a fork until blended. Add this to the flour mixture: stir with a spoon until mixed.

♥ Pour mixture into the greased pan. Place pan in the oven and bake for 35 minutes or until golden.

♥ Remove pan from the oven. Serve warm, with butter. This is great when served with Chilly's Chili.

Benny Beanie's™ Nutritional Facts (per serving):
Calories 191; Fat 7g (Saturated 1g); Cholesterol 39mg;
Sodium 306mg; Carbohydrate 28g; Protein 5g

Wake up in the morning to the smell of bread!
(Assuming Mom got out of bed.)
Caw searched the backroads for this fare
Its awesome taste gave the crow a scare!

the Grit's Pit

 Caw the Crow

ERIN'S IRISH SODA BREAD MUFFINS

18 Servings

INGREDIENTS

- 4   cups flour
- 1   teaspoon salt
- 1   teaspoon baking soda
- 1   teaspoon cream of tartar
- 4   tablespoons sugar
- 1   stick butter, softened
- 2   eggs
- 1-3/4 cups buttermilk
- 3/4 cup raisins

A FOOD TIP FROM NIP & ZIP

Back in the old country (what old country?), Nip and Zip used to enjoy Irish Soda Bread Muffins while sipping milk in the gazebo. Their only criticism of these delicious muffins (and everything else they get their claws on) is: "Makes too many crumbs."

HOW TO MAKE 'EM

♥ Preheat oven to 350°.

♥ In a medium mixing bowl, add flour, salt, baking soda, cream of tartar and sugar. Mix well.

♥ Add butter and raisins to the dry ingredients.

♥ Beat eggs, and add with buttermilk to the flour mixture. Mix until well blended.

♥ Line muffin tins with paper cups, or grease tins with butter. Pour batter into prepared tins, filling 2/3 full.

♥ Bake muffins for 30 minutes.

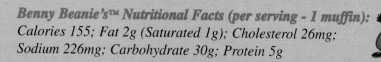

Benny Beanie's™ Nutritional Facts (per serving - 1 muffin):
Calories 155; Fat 2g (Saturated 1g); Cholesterol 26mg;
Sodium 226mg; Carbohydrate 30g; Protein 5g

Aye, here's a tempting Irish treat,
Why, Laddie, it's good enough to eat!
Can you taste the thick, fresh buttermilk?
It goes down quick and smooth as silk!

Erin the Irish Teddy

CRANBERRY TEDDY'S CRANBERRY MUFFINS

18 Servings

INGREDIENTS

- 2 cups flour
- 1 cup sugar
- 1-1/2 teaspoons baking powder
- 1/2 teaspoon baking soda
- 1/2 teaspoon nutmeg
- 1 teaspoon cinnamon
- 1/2 teaspoon ginger
- 1/2 cup butter or margarine
- 3/4 cup orange juice
- 1 tablespoon vanilla
- 2 eggs
- 1-1/2 cups cranberries
- 1 cup nuts, chopped

A FOOD TIP FROM NIP & ZIP

Both Nip and Zip recommend the use of New Jersey Cranberries if you want this recipe to turn our purr-fect. Because cranberries are not always in season, you might want to store a 50 gallon jug (or two) in your fruit cellar.

HOW TO MAKE 'EM

♥ Mix the first seven ingredients together in a large bowl.

♥ Add 1/2 cup of butter/margarine to the bowl and stir well with a fork.

♥ The batter will be very lumpy.

♥ Stir in the juice, vanilla, and eggs.

♥ Lightly mix in cranberries and nuts.

♥ Spoon into paper-lined muffin cups, filling about 3/4 full.

♥ Bake at 350° for 25 minutes.

Benny Beanie's™ Nutritional Facts (per serving - 1 muffin):
Calories 208; Fat 10g (Saturated 4g); Cholesterol 37mg;
Sodium 113mg; Carbohydrate 26g; Protein 4g

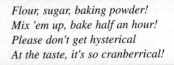

Flour, sugar, baking powder!
Mix 'em up, bake half an hour!
Please don't get hysterical
At the taste, it's so cranberrical!

Cranberry Teddy

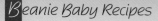

ALLY'S "SNAPPY" GINGER COOKIES

18 Servings

INGREDIENTS

2/3   cup vegetable oil

1   cup sugar

1   whole egg, beaten

4   tablespoons molasses, natural light

2   cups flour, all purpose

2   teaspoons baking soda

1/2   teaspoon salt

1   teaspoon cinnamon

1   teaspoon ginger, ground

A FOOD TIP FROM NIP & ZIP

According to Nip, Ally's "Snappy" Ginger Cookies taste best with a glass (or bowl) of cold milk. Nip recommends rolling around on your back for 5 to 6 minutes before eating a cookie. Playing the devil's advo-cat, Zip prefers Ally's Ginger Cookies dry, claiming the cookie gourmet will experience a richer, fuller flavor by chewing slowly on a clean palate.

HOW TO MAKE 'EM

♥ Preheat oven to 350°.

♥ In a large mixing bowl, add all of the above ingredients, and mix well.

♥ Roll dough into balls, about 3/4 teaspoons each.

♥ In a small bowl, place 1/2 cup of granulated sugar. Roll each ball in sugar, and place on an ungreased cookie sheet, about 2 inches apart.

♥ Bake for 9-11 minutes. Makes approximately 6 dozen cookies.

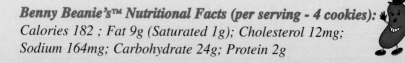

Benny Beanie's™ Nutritional Facts (per serving - 4 cookies):
Calories 182 ; Fat 9g (Saturated 1g); Cholesterol 12mg;
Sodium 164mg; Carbohydrate 24g; Protein 2g

Ally the 'gator was taking a tally
Of afternoon snacks that were right up his alley
He decided that cookies were really his fave
Try 'em and see if you give these a rave!

Ally the Aligator

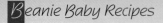
BONES' PAINTED SUGAR COOKIES

30 Servings

INGREDIENTS

- 1/2 cup softened butter
- 1 cup sugar
- 1 egg
- 1 teaspoon vanilla
- 1/4 teaspoon almond extract
- 1/2 teaspoon salt
- 2 teaspoons baking powder
- 2 cups flour

A FOOD TIP FROM NIP & ZIP

Zip was shocked at how fantastic these sugary dog cookies taste. He quickly convinced his pal, Nip, to try some. At first, Nip was noncommittal. But he knew we really had something when he opened his mouth and a loud bark came out!

HOW TO MAKE 'EM

♥ Preheat oven to 400°.

♥ Mix together butter and sugar. Blend in egg, vanilla, and almond extract. Add salt, baking powder, flour. Mix well.

♥ Roll out on lightly floured board, about 1/4" thickness. Use assorted cookie cutters. Place on ungreased baking sheets.

♥ Bake approx. 7-9 minutes.

♥ **For Glaze:** Mix 3-4 teaspoons of milk, to 3/4 cup sifted confectioners sugar, add a drop of vanilla. Mix well to desired consistency, may need to add more milk. Add food coloring for variety. Paint on with paint brush, or make thicker and pipe on with decorating bag/tubes.

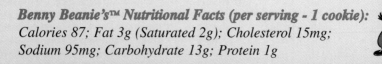

Benny Beanie's™ Nutritional Facts (per serving - 1 cookie): Calories 87; Fat 3g (Saturated 2g); Cholesterol 15mg; Sodium 95mg; Carbohydrate 13g; Protein 1g

These cookies are as cute as Bones
They taste a lot like ice cream cones,
Keep 'em on hand for a nice surprise
The neighborhood dogs won't believe their eyes!

CHIP'S CHOCOLATE CHIP COOKIE CUPS

24 Servings

INGREDIENTS

18   ounces refrigerated chocolate chip cookie dough

24   chocolate candy kisses, or mini marshmallows mixed with nuts and chocolate chips

peanut butter cups

M&Ms, regular or mini

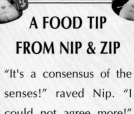

A FOOD TIP FROM NIP & ZIP

"It's a consensus of the senses!" raved Nip. "I could not agree more!" yelped Zip. "Chip's cookie cups are arguably the most sense-sational smell toys since catnip scented rubber mice!"

HOW TO MAKE 'EM

♥ Preheat oven to 375°.

♥ Line miniature muffin pans with small paper baking cups.

♥ Open package of chocolate chip cookie dough as directed, and scoop level tablespoon of dough into each muffin cup.

♥ Place pan on the center rack in oven and bake 12-14 minutes or until golden.

♥ Carefully remove cookies from oven. Immediately place one kiss, or other candy into each cup, gently press down.

♥ Return to oven and bake 1-2 minutes longer, just so the candy begins to melt.

♥ Remove from oven, let cool slightly in the pan, then remove from muffin tin, and cool completely.

Benny Beanie's™ Nutritional Facts (per serving - 1 cookie cup):
Calories 140; Fat 6g (Saturated 2g); Cholesterol 10mg;
Sodium 100mg; Carbohydrate 20g; Protein 2g

One day Chip got a great idea.
"Chocolate Chip Cookie Cups" rang in his ear.
"If I can think 'em, I can make 'em."
So here they are, now you can bake 'em!

Chip the Cat

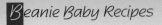

MYSTIC'S FRESH FRUIT PIZZA COOKIE

10 Servings

INGREDIENTS

- 1 package (20 oz.) refrigerated cookie dough
- 1 8 oz. package cream cheese
- 1/3 cup sugar
- 1 teaspoon vanilla extract
- 1 20 oz. can sliced pineapple
- 1 peeled and sliced banana
- 1 peeled and sliced kiwi
- 1/4 cup raspberries (optional)
- 1/4 cup apricot jam, melted

A FOOD TIP FROM NIP & ZIP

Nip and Zip actually consulted with Julia Roberts (they thought she was Julia Childs) in order to evaluate our pizza. Their conclusion: Mystic's Pizza is so cool it will satisfy the appetite of either a pretty woman or a cool cat!

HOW TO MAKE 'EM

♥ Preheat oven to 350°.

♥ Press cookie dough onto 14-inch pizza pan.

♥ Bake in oven for 12 to 15 minutes until browned and puffed. Cool.

♥ Beat the cream cheese until softened, add sugar and vanilla until blended. Spread over cooled cookie.

♥ Arrange canned pineapple around outer edge of cream cheese.

♥ Arrange kiwi slightly overlapping pineapple. Continue with banana and raspberries in center.

♥ Melt apricot jam in a small saucepan. Lightly spoon, or brush jam over the fruit.

♥ Cut into wedges, and serve. Refrigerate uneaten pizza.

Benny Beanie's™ Nutritional Facts (per serving - 1 slice):
Calories 411; Fat 18g (Saturated 5g); Cholesterol 25mg;
Sodium 293mg; Carbohydrate 59g; Protein 4g

**Mystic
theUnicorn
(Fine Yarn)**

**Mystic
(Tan Horn)**

**Mystic
(Striped Horn)**

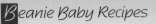
PEANUT'S PEANUTTY COOKIES

18 Servings

INGREDIENTS

1-1/2	cups flour
1/4	teaspoon salt
1/2	teaspoon baking soda
1/2	cup butter, softened
3/4	cup peanut butter, creamy or chunky
1/2	cup sugar
1/2	cup light brown sugar, lightly packed
1/2	teaspoon vanilla extract
1	large egg

A FOOD TIP FROM NIP & ZIP

Do you seem to have a problem with peanut butter sticking to your teeth? Zip has the solution. After eating these irresistible cookies, brush your teeth 10 times! Nip has a better idea. Bake a toothbrush right into the batter!

HOW TO MAKE 'EM

♥ Preheat oven to 350°.

♥ In a small bowl, mix flour, salt and baking soda.

♥ In a medium bowl, beat butter, peanut butter, both of the sugars, and vanilla with an electric mixer on medium high speed for about 1 minute, or until fluffy. Beat in egg until blended.

♥ With the mixer on low, add flour mixture, and beat until well blended.

♥ Lightly grease the cookie sheets.

♥ Take 2 level tablespoons full of dough and roll into 1-1/2 inch balls. Place on cookie sheets 2 inches apart. With the tines of a fork, press down on each cookie to make a crisscross pattern.

♥ Bake 16-18 minutes or until golden around the edges. Remove from cookie sheet to cool.

Benny Beanie's™ Nutritional Facts (per serving - 1 cookie):
Calories 190; Fat 11g (Saturated 4g); Cholesterol 26mg;
Sodium 100mg; Carbohydrate 19g; Protein 4g

They say an elephant never forgets
Peanut says he has no regrets.
To protect his cookies, he'll step on you
Then you'll be peanut butter, too!

Peanut the Elephant

ROYAL PEANUT'S ELEGANT ELEPHANT EARS

12 Servings

INGREDIENTS

1　16 oz. package puff pastry dough
1/2　cup sugar

HOW TO MAKE 'EM

♥ Following directions on package of frozen puff pastry dough, thaw at room temperature for about 30 minutes.
♥ Gently unfold pastry sheets.
♥ Roll and shape dough on a lightly floured surface, so pastry won't stick.
♥ Roll into a rectangle about 8"x10" wide and 1/8 thick. The sheet should be close to that size from the time you unwrap it. If any cracks develop in the pastry, sprinkle with water and press together to seal. Cut edges so they are even.
♥ Sprinkle top of the pastry with a light coating of sugar.
♥ Roll each long end to the middle of the pastry rectangle, making sure the pastry is even.
♥ Cut crosswise into about 3/8" slices.
♥ Place baking sheets on table and lightly sprinkle with water.
♥ Dip both sides of elephant ears in sugar, and place 3 inches apart on sheets. Cover and refrigerate at least 1 hour.
♥ Preheat oven to 400°.
♥ Bake elephant ears for about 5-6 minutes until bottoms begin to brown. Remove quickly from oven and turn ears over, put back into the oven and bake 3-4 minutes more or until the tops are slightly browned, but not burned.
♥ Cool on wire racks, and store in airtight container.
♥ Makes approximately 48 tiny elephant ears.

A FOOD TIP FROM NIP & ZIP

Is there anything more aromatic than baked elephant ears? (Not the real thing, silly!) When Nip and Zip smelled these snacks heating up in the Beanie oven, their own ears (and noses) perked up. They quickly rushed to the source of the food and uncapped two bottles of Yoo Hoo.

Benny Beanie's™ *Nutritional Facts (per serving - 4 ears):*
Calories 193; Fat 11g (Saturated 3g); Cholesterol 0mg;
Sodium 180mg; Carbohydrate 22g; Protein 2g

One day, before his afternoon snack,
Dark blue Peanut blew his nose
A piercing whistle shook his back
And made his ears drop to his toes!

Peanut the Elephant

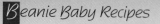

VALENTINO'S LINZER TARTS

30 Servings

INGREDIENTS

1-1/2	cups butter
1	cup sugar
2	eggs
1	teaspoon vanilla extract
1	12 oz. package whole almonds, blanched and finely ground
3-1/3	cups cake flour, sifted
1	teaspoon baking powder
1	teaspoon ground cinnamon
3/4	cup raspberry preserves
1/4	cup powdered sugar

A FOOD TIP FROM NIP & ZIP

A dozen red roses and a dozen Valentino Linzer Tarts are just the right combination to win the heart of the object of your affection: Mom, Dad, girlfriend or boyfriend, your favorite TV crush, the Secretary-General of the United Nations, whoever...

HOW TO MAKE 'EM

♥ Preheat oven to 350°.

♥ In a mixing bowl, cream butter; gradually add 1 cup of sugar, beating until light. Add eggs and vanilla, beating well; stir in ground almonds, mixing well.

♥ In another bowl, sift together flour, baking powder, and cinnamon; slowly, add to the butter mixture, stirring well. Divide dough into four equal pieces; cover and refrigerate at least 3 hours.

♥ Roll one portion of dough to 1/4-inch thickness between 2 pieces of waxed paper. Keep remaining dough refrigerated until ready to use. Cut with a 2-inch heart shaped cookie cutter; place half of cookies on lightly greased cookie sheets. Cut out centers of remaining cookies, using a 3/4-inch round cutter or a smaller heart-shaped cutter. Place on greased cookie sheets.

♥ Bake for 10-12 minutes. Remove cookies to wire racks to cool. Repeat procedure with remaining dough.

♥ Spread a small amount of jam on bottom of each solid cookie. Top with the remaining cookie, bottom sides down, to make sandwiches. Sift powdered sugar over the tops. Fill cut-outs with jam. Store in airtight containers.

♥ Makes about 30 cookies.

Benny Beanie's™ Nutritional Facts (per serving - 1 cookie):
Calories 257; Fat 16g (Saturated 16g); Cholesterol 39mg;
Sodium 112mg; Carbohydrate 25g; Protein 4g

There is a day in February
When lovers leap from morn till night
And Valentino's Linzer tarts
Fill every heart with sheer delight.

Valentino the Teddy Bear

ZIGGY & BLIZZARD'S BLACK & WHITE COOKIES

36 Servings

INGREDIENTS

1-1/2	cups sugar
1	cup butter, softened
4	eggs
1	cup milk
1/2	teaspoon vanilla
1/4	teaspoon lemon extract
2-1/2	cups all purpose flour
2-3/4	cups cake flour
1	teaspoon baking powder
1/2	teaspoon salt

FROSTING

4	cups confectioners sugar
1/4	cup boiling water
1	ounce semisweet chocolate
1/4	teaspoon vanilla

A FOOD TIP FROM NIP & ZIP

As usual, the food cats don't see catseye-to-catseye. Understandably, Zip recommends cutting these cookies in half and discarding the white portion. Unable to control his animalistic desires, Nip scrambles for any uneaten food, impartial to its color. He is, however, campaigning for a recipe for Black and Gold cookies.

HOW TO MAKE 'EM

♥ Preheat oven to 375°.

♥ Grease 2 cookie sheets and put aside until needed.

♥ In a large bowl, add sugar and butter, and mix to combine, either by hand or with an electric mixer. Beat until fluffy. Add eggs, milk, vanilla and lemon extracts, and mix until very smooth.

♥ In another bowl, mix both flours, baking powder and salt and mix until combined. Add dry ingredients to the butter mixture. Mix well.

♥ Using a large tablespoon, drop spoonfuls of batter on to the greased cookie sheets, leaving about 2 inches between each cookie.

♥ Bake cookies for about 20 to 25 minutes, or until edges begin to brown. Cool cookies completely, before you begin to ice them.

♥ Begin to make the frosting by placing all of the confectioners sugar into a large bowl. Boil 1/4 cup of water and gradually add to the sugar, stir constantly until the mixture is smooth and quite thick.

♥ Put half of the frosting in the top part of a double boiler and set over simmering water. Add semisweet chocolate, and stir until all of the chocolate has melted, and the frosting is very smooth. Remove this pan from the heat and stir again.

♥ Using a brush or a spoon, coat half of each cookie with chocolate frosting, and then with vanilla frosting. Stir frosting from time to time if it begins to harden.

Benny Beanie's™ Nutritional Facts (per serving - 1 cookie):
Calories 210; Fat 6g (Saturated 4g); Cholesterol 38mg;
Sodium 104mg; Carbohydrate 36g; Protein 3g

No color barriers on this page
Black and white Beanies are all the rage!
So why not have a cookie fest
To show the world that life is blessed?

Blizzard the Tiger

Ziggy the Zebra

Delectable
Desserts

Ice Cream
Delights

Fruits &
Drinks

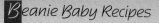
BROWNIE'S FAMOUS BROWNIES

16 Servings

INGREDIENTS

- 2 ounces unsweetened chocolate
- 1/2 cup butter, softened
- 1 cup sugar
- 2 eggs
- 1/2 cup flour
- 1 pinch salt
- 1 cup nuts, chopped
- 1/2 teaspoon vanilla

A FOOD TIP FROM NIP & ZIP

Nip likes to squirt a medium size blob of whipped cream on top of his brownies, then lick it off, then squirt another blob, lick it off, and so on. Zip had to take away his can of whipped cream to get him to admit that the Brownie itself is the highlight!

HOW TO MAKE 'EM

♥ Preheat oven to 350°.

♥ Grease 8" square pan.

♥ Melt chocolate over hot water in double boiler or in microwave.

♥ In a large mixing bowl, cream butter, until soft; gradually add in sugar, and beat until mixture is fluffy. (I prefer to do this by hand.)

♥ Add eggs one at a time, beating after each addition.

♥ In a medium mixing bowl, sift flour with salt, and stir into mixture.

♥ Stir in nuts, melted chocolate and vanilla.

♥ Spread mixture in the prepared pan, and bake in preheated oven for 25-30 minutes or until a dull crust has formed.

♥ Cool slightly and cut into squares.

Benny Beanie's™ Nutritional Facts (per serving - 1 brownie): Calories 202; Fat 13g (Saturated 5g); Cholesterol 42mg; Sodium 212mg; Carbohydrate 19g; Protein 3g

Not to be confused with Famous Amos,
Brownie's Famous are the best
If you think that food can't tame us,
Put these babies to the test!

Brownie the Bear

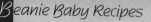

BEANIE BUNNIES' FAVORITE CARROT CAKE

16 Servings

INGREDIENTS

2   cups flour
2   teaspoons baking soda
2   teaspoons cinnamon
2   cups sugar
1   teaspoon salt
4   eggs
1   cup vegetable oil
4   cups grated carrots
1/2   cup chopped pecans
4   tablespoons butter, softened
6   ounces cream cheese, softened
4   cups powdered sugar
1   teaspoon vanilla

A FOOD TIP FROM NIP & ZIP

Floppity, Hippity and Hoppity eat their carrot cake standing up. Ears eats his lying flat on his belly! It's a little uncomfortable, but that's the price Ears has to pay for being a Beanie Baby bunny rabbit.

HOW TO MAKE 'EM

♥ Preheat oven to 350°.

♥ Prepare pans by greasing and flouring either, (2) 9" round pans, or (1) 13" x 9" pan.

♥ In a large bowl, mix together flour, baking soda, cinnamon, sugar and salt.

♥ In a small bowl, beat eggs until frothy, add oil and mix. Add to the flour mixture, mix thoroughly with a spoon.

♥ Stir in grated carrots and pecans.

♥ Pour into the prepared pans, and bake 30-35 minutes.

♥ Remove cake from oven and cool on wire rack.

♥ Frost cake with cream cheese frosting.

CREAM CHEESE FROSTING:

♥ In a large bowl, blend butter with cream cheese. Beat in about 4 cups of powdered sugar, until creamy. Add 1 teaspoon vanilla. Mix well.

Benny Beanie's™ Nutritional Facts (per serving - 1 square):
Calories 519; Fat 24g (Saturated 6g); Cholesterol 73mg;
Sodium 335mg; Carbohydrate 71g; Protein 5g

"Eh, What's Up Doc?" the Bunnies question,
They like to eat cake with their spoons,
Ten slices give them indigestion
And the sugar drives them Looney Toons!

Hoppity the Bunny

Floppity the Bunny

Hippity the Bunny

Ears the Bunny

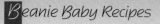
CHOCOLATE'S CHOCOLATE "MOOSE"

4 Servings

INGREDIENTS

8	ounces semisweet chocolate
2-1/2	tablespoons confectioners sugar
2	egg yolks (no whites, see how to separate in Cooking Terms)
2	tablespoons strong coffee
1	tablespoons water
1-1/4	cups whipping cream

A FOOD TIP FROM NIP & ZIP

Does a moose really eat chocolate? This question was carefully researched by Nip in the deep forests of Utah, Maine and Brazil. After tracking for weeks, Nip came to the same conclusion as Zip. It's hard to find a Moose when you need one. So they asked a Brazilian forest ranger, who did not speak English.

HOW TO MAKE 'EM

♥ Put the chocolate in the top part of a double boiler and set over simmering water.

♥ Stir the chocolate for 4-5 minutes, or until it has melted.

♥ Add the sugar and egg yolks only, to the chocolate, and stir with a whisk or fork.

♥ Make regular or instant coffee in a small cup. Add 2 tablespoons of this to the chocolate mixture, along with 1 tablespoon of water and stir with the whisk.

♥ Remove top part of the double boiler from the heat and set aside.

♥ In a medium bowl, add the cream and whip on high speed until the cream forms soft peaks. Remove about 1/2 cup and set aside in the refrigerator.

♥ Gently add the rest of cream to the chocolate mixture. Do not stir, but "fold" into the chocolate mixture.

♥ Spoon the mousse into 4 individual serving dishes, or one large dish.

♥ Refrigerate at least 2 hours.

♥ Top with remaining 1/2 cup of whipped cream. Decorate with either mandarin oranges, or fruit of your choice.

Benny Beanie's™ Nutritional Facts (per serving):
Calories 612; Fat 50g (Saturated 29g); Cholesterol 205mg;
Sodium 33mg; Carbohydrate 35g; Protein 5g

Take off your antlers, rest your bones
Shove some chocolate between your lips
Look in the mirror, when you're alone,
Where did it go? It's on your hips!

Chocolate the Moose

KIWI'S TROPICAL SHORTCAKE

6 Servings

INGREDIENTS

2-1/3   cups biscuit mix
1/2   cup milk
3-1/2   tablespoons sugar
3   tablespoons margarine or butter, melted
3   peeled and sliced kiwis
1   peeled and sliced banana
1   pint strawberries or raspberries
1   6 oz. can pineapple, cubed
1   pint blueberries
whipped cream or whipped topping

HOW TO MAKE 'EM

♥ Preheat oven to 425°.

♥ In a medium sized mixing bowl, add biscuit mix, milk, sugar and melted butter. Stir until a soft dough forms.

♥ Remove dough from bowl and place on a lightly floured surface. Knead the dough about 10 times. Roll out the dough to a 1/2" thickness. Cut with a 3" round cookie cutter. You can also use a rim of a drinking glass – be careful when doing this, as the glass could break. Place biscuits on an ungreased cookie sheet.

♥ Bake 10 -12 minutes. until lightly golden.

♥ Prepare fruit by washing, peeling and slicing if necessary; and mix together in a bowl. Keep the fruit refrigerated.

♥ When biscuits have cooled and you are ready to serve your guests, split each shortcake in half lengthwise.

♥ Place bottom half of the biscuit on each plate. Top with a few tablespoons of whipped cream, followed by a few spoonfuls of fruit. Top this with the other half of biscuit and more whipped cream and fruit.

A FOOD TIP FROM NIP & ZIP

While searching for a moose in the jungles of Brazil, Nip and Zip happened to come across a tribe of native Kiwis. Amazingly, the leader of the pack (shown to right) possessed authentic photos of a moose eating chocolate. (See Recipe #39 Food Tip.)

Benny Beanie's™ Nutritional Facts (per serving - 1 shortcake):
Calories 485; Fat 24g (Saturated 10g); Cholesterol 40mg;
Sodium 750mg; Carbohydrate 64g; Protein 5g

Kiwi, Kiwi, chirping bright
In the forests of the night
Only a Kiwi could be merrier
About shortcake so strawberrier!

 Kiwi the Toucan

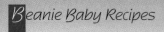

REX'S ROCKY ROAD

32 Servings

INGREDIENTS

2	8 ounces bars (16 oz.) milk chocolate, cut up
2-1/2	cups tiny white marshmallows
3/4	cup chopped walnuts
	butter

HOW TO MAKE 'EM

♥ Line an 8x8x2 inch baking pan with foil – making sure foil goes over the edges of the pan. Rub butter on the foil to prevent candy from sticking.

♥ Heat milk chocolate in a medium sauce pan over very low heat, making sure to stir constantly until melted. Turn off the heat and stir in marshmallows and chopped nuts. Spread mixture into foil lined pan.

♥ Place pan in the refrigerator and chill about 40 minutes until firm. When firm use foil to lift candy from pan; cut candy into small squares about 1" each. Store in covered container – makes about 64 pieces.

A FOOD TIP FROM NIP & ZIP

Kids across America are dying to hear the musical version of our song, "The Beanie Baby Dinosaur Stomp (Chomp! Chomp! Chomp! Chomp!)"* While you're waiting to "Do The Rex!" you can now chomp on his favorite dessert. Dig in, fellow Beanie lovers! (*Lyrics in the 1998 Beanie Baby Handbook.)

Benny Beanie's™ Nutritional Facts (per serving - 2 pieces):
Calories 109; Fat 6g (Saturated 3g); Cholesterol 3mg;
Sodium 15mg; Carbohydrate 11g; Protein 2g

Rex the Tyrannosaurus

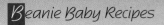
SPEEDY'S CARAMEL PECAN "TURTLES"

25 Servings

INGREDIENTS

- 2 cups pecan halves, lightly toasted
- 7 ounces caramel candies, about 25 pieces
- 1 tablespoon water
- 6 ounces milk or semisweet chocolate chips

A FOOD TIP FROM NIP & ZIP

Nip asked Speedy if he could hitch a ride on his back while he munched on a few caramel pecan turtles. "Just as long as you don't decide you want turtle soup for dinner," replied the clever hardback. "If you get a hankering for the genuine article, just remember my Teenage Mutant Ninja brothers are only a phone call away."

HOW TO MAKE 'EM

♥ Spread pecan halves in a single layer on a shallow baking pan. Toast in 350° oven, for about 7 minutes, stirring once or twice.

♥ Line a baking sheet with aluminum foil. Lightly coat the foil with butter. Arrange pecans on the prepared baking sheet in groups of 5, placing the flat side down, to form head, feet and legs. Set baking sheet aside.

♥ In a heavy sauce pan, combine caramels and water. Cook on very low heat, stirring constantly, until the caramels become smooth. Or put caramels in a microwavable container with water. Place in microwave, and heat on high 1 minute. Stir, and return to microwave, if needed, for 30 seconds.

♥ Remove pan from the heat. Drop 1 teaspoon of caramel onto each group of pecans, making sure head, arms and legs are all attached. Cool for about 15 minutes or until caramel becomes firm.

♥ In a small saucepan, over low heat, melt chocolate, until smooth. Stir constantly to avoid burning. This can also be done in a microwave oven. Place in microwavable container for 1-2 minutes. Make sure not to burn chocolate, as this can happen very quickly. Spoon about 1 teaspoon of chocolate over the tops of each caramel center, spread with a butter knife.

♥ To make eyes, place two small dots of chocolate on one pecan, on each turtle, using a toothpick. Let stand, until chocolate becomes hardened. Remove from baking sheet, store in covered container.

Benny Beanie's™ Nutritional Facts (per serving - 1 turtle):
Calories 134; Fat 9g (Saturated 2g); Cholesterol 0mg;
Sodium 18mg; Carbohydrate 12g; Protein 1g

"Slow and steady wins the race,"
Or so the saying goes.
Hey, look, it's true! That's Speedy's face!
He's winning by a turtle nose!

Speedy the Turtle

SPINNER & WEB'S CREEPY-CRAWLER CUPCAKES

18 Servings

INGREDIENTS

- 1   18.25 oz. package devils food cake mix
- 1   16 oz. can chocolate frosting
- 1   cup chocolate sprinkles
- 9   marshmallows, halved
- 2   bunches black licorice, strings
- 36 pieces round colored candies

HOW TO MAKE 'EM

♥ Heat oven to 350°. Line 18 muffin cups with paper liners. Prepare batter according to directions on devils food cake mix, and divide evenly among cups. Bake as directed. Remove cupcakes from baking tin, and cool .

♥ Frost cupcakes. Place marshmallow half on the edge of each cupcake; frost marshmallow.

♥ Dip each frosted cupcake in the chocolate sprinkles,until well coated.

♥ For each spider cupcake, cut eight 4" long pieces of licorice for legs and two 1-1/2" pieces for antennae. Insert longer pieces into the spider's body (4 on each side); poke shorter pieces into marshmallow heads. For eyes, place 2 candies below antennae.

A FOOD TIP FROM NIP & ZIP

Zip wants you to know that the silly poem on the opposite page is just a joke from Les and Sue. In order to prove that there's nothing strange about Spinner and Web's cupcakes, he and Nip made a personal sacrifice. They spent a whole weekend eating nothing but Creepy-Crawlers!

Benny Beanie's™ Nutritional Facts (per serving - 1 cupcake): Calories 294; Fat 14g (Saturated 4g); Cholesterol 37mg; Sodium 314mg; Carbohydrate 39g; Protein 3g

Spinner the Spider

Web the Spider

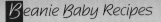
TEENIE BEANIES' TEENIE WEENIE CHEESECAKES

30 Servings

INGREDIENTS

- 30 vanilla wafer cookies, 1 box
- 4 8 oz. packages cream cheese, softened at room temperature
- 1 cup sugar
- 2 tablespoons vanilla
- 4 eggs

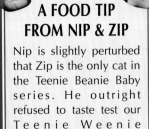

A FOOD TIP FROM NIP & ZIP

Nip is slightly perturbed that Zip is the only cat in the Teenie Beanie Baby series. He outright refused to taste test our Teenie Weenie Cheesecakes! So Zip ate every last one of them, which he reported is a great way to dislodge furballs!

HOW TO MAKE 'EM

♥ Preheat oven to 350°.

♥ In a large mixing bowl add cream cheese, mix a little with a fork until softened. Add sugar, eggs and vanilla.

♥ Beat until creamy, using a mixer on low speed, or by hand, mixing well so no huge lumps remain.

♥ Place paper muffin liners into muffin tins (or use foil muffin cups.) In each cup place 1 vanilla wafer cookie.

♥ Pour cream cheese mixture over the cookie, filling 3/4 or less, full.

♥ Bake for 20-25 minutes.

♥ Remove from oven and cool. Refrigerate.

♥ Can be eaten as is, or add toppings, either canned or fresh fruit is delicious. Or make marzipan fruits, or Teenie Beanies as shown.

♥ Makes 30 cheesecakes (this recipe can easily be divided in half to make 15 cakes.)

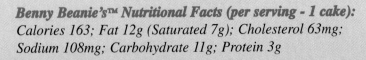

Benny Beanie's™ Nutritional Facts (per serving - 1 cake):
Calories 163; Fat 12g (Saturated 7g); Cholesterol 63mg;
Sodium 108mg; Carbohydrate 11g; Protein 3g

So little and so good to eat
Our Teenie Cheesecakes can't be beat
You won't gain weight if you just have one
The problem is, they're too much fun!

Teenie Beanies: Snort, Speedy, Pinky, Patti, Seamore, Lizzy, Goldie, Chops, Chocolate, Quacks

LIBEARTY, LEFTY & RIGHTY'S POLITICAL PIE

8 Servings

INGREDIENTS

1   quart strawberry ice cream, softened
1   ready made graham cracker pie crust
1   pint strawberries
1   pint blueberries
1   cup mini marshmallows
1   cup whipped topping

HOW TO MAKE 'EM

♥ Fill graham cracker crust with strawberry ice cream. Cover and place in freezer until firm about 1 hour.

♥ Remove pie from freezer. Using a table knife frost the entire top of the pie with whipped topping.

♥ Arrange blueberries, strawberries and mini marshmallows in any pattern you wish. Strawberries can remain whole, or can be sliced, depending on your design.

♥ Place pie carefully on a cookie sheet and put back in to the freezer. Freeze until firm, or over nite.

♥ To serve, remove from freezer for about 5-10 minutes. Slice and serve.

A FOOD TIP FROM NIP & ZIP

Nip and Zip finally agree on something. "Political Pie" should be adopted as America's national dessert. They also agree that a few extra scoops of chocolate chip wouldn't hurt either!

Benny Beanie's™ Nutritional Facts (per serving - 1 slice):
Calories 297; Fat 17g (Saturated 5g); Cholesterol 34mg; Sodium 122mg; Carbohydrate 37g; Protein 7g

America is our favorite place
Even with ice cream on our face!
We raise the flag, and proudly salute
These Beanie Babies. Aren't they cute?

RETIRED Libearty the Bear

RETIRED Righty the Elephant

RETIRED Lefty the Donkey

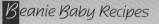
PINKY'S FLAMINGO FLAMBÉ

2 Servings

INGREDIENTS

1   pint strawberry ice cream
    whipped cream
1   cup strawberry ice cream topping
    chopped bubble gum
    maraschino cherries
    sparkler candles

HOW TO MAKE 'EM

♥ Place two large scoops of ice cream into each bowl.

♥ Top with strawberry topping, whipped cream, cherry and chopped bubble gum.

♥ Place sparkler candles into ice cream. Have an adult light the candles, serve immediately.

♥ Makes two large servings.

A FOOD TIP FROM NIP & ZIP

Zip warned Nip to be careful when he tried to light one of the candles on this pink flavor festival. After three failed attempts, Nip decided to ask his dad to strike the match for him. Then the whole family jumped on top of the table and made a giant mess!

Benny Beanie's™ Nutritional Facts (per serving):
Calories 410; Fat 15g (Saturated 9g); Cholesterol 58mg; Sodium 130mg; Carbohydrate 70g; Protein 5g

Hope you like the color pink!
Hope you like our maraschinies!
Wash your hands in the kitchen sink
And celebrate with all your Beanies!

Pinky the Flamingo

SEAMORE'S ARCTIC S'MORES

6 Servings

INGREDIENTS

- 6   single serving (4 oz. size) graham cracker crusts
-    5 oz. milk chocolate bar, or chips
- 1/2   cup marshmallow cream
- 1   pint vanilla ice cream
-    whipped cream, or non dairy topping
- 6   maraschino cherries

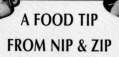

A FOOD TIP FROM NIP & ZIP

Nip posed the obvious question to Zip: "After you eat these, don't you want some more?" Zip's witty reply: "I wouldn't settle for anything less." Both cats recommend a few heaping teaspoons of hot fudge to round out the flavor.

HOW TO MAKE 'EM

♥ Melt 5 ounces of milk, or semisweet chocolate, in a microwaveable container for 1 to 1-1/2 minutes, or, on the stove in a small saucepan, over low heat. (Be very careful not to over cook, as chocolate burns very quickly.)

♥ In the bottom of each crust place about 2 tablespoons of melted chocolate, and very carefully, with the back of a spoon, coat the bottom and sides of each crust. Place the 6 crusts on a small baking sheet, and place in refrigerator for about 15 minutes, or until chocolate hardens.

♥ When the chocolate has hardened, spoon a heaping tablespoon of marshmallow cream into each pie. Spread to coat the bottoms.

♥ Remove vanilla ice cream from the freezer, and let sit at room temperature until soft enough to scoop. Fill each crust with ice cream, cover with plastic wrap or wax paper, and return the crusts to the freezer, to harden.

♥ Freeze until ready to serve.

♥ When ready to serve, top each S'more with whipped cream or non dairy whipped topping, and a cherry.

Benny Beanie's™ Nutritional Facts (per serving - 1 s'more):
Calories 400; Fat 20g (Saturated 7g); Cholesterol 7mg;
Sodium 213mg; Carbohydrate 45g; Protein 7g

As icy and exciting as the Titanic,
Seamore's S'Mores are great for a picnic,
Take some along on a bobsled ride,
Makes you feel all warm and fuzzy inside!

Jolly the Walrus

Seamore the Seal

Tusk the Walrus

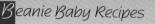
SNOWBALL'S SNOWBALLS

6 Servings

INGREDIENTS

1   quart vanilla ice cream
2   cups shredded coconut
1   cup chocolate syrup

HOW TO MAKE 'EM

♥ Remove vanilla ice cream from freezer, and put into refrigerator, for about 15 minutes, until it is soft enough to scoop.

♥ Put coconut in flat bowl.

♥ With a scooper, scoop large balls of ice cream, trying to keep a round shape.

♥ Using two forks, roll in coconut, until completely covered. Mold with clean hands, to keep round appearance.

♥ Place on a small baking sheet in your freezer. Cover with plastic wrap to prevent the coconut from drying out. Freeze at least 2 hours.

♥ To serve, place 1 "Snowball" on each plate, and drizzle with chocolate sauce. Serve with a cookie, or fresh fruit on the side.

A FOOD TIP FROM NIP & ZIP

Nip and Zip think that Snowball's Snowballs are more fun than a ball of yarn. Of course, they prefer mouse-flavored ice cream (yuk) to vanilla, and have written several letters to Baskin-Robbins requesting this culinary oddity.

Benny Beanie's™ Nutritional Facts (per serving):
Calories 432; Fat 20g (Saturated 15g); Cholesterol 44mg;
Sodium 141mg; Carbohydrate 59g; Protein 5g

Roll a snowball down a hill,
Watch it grow, it's such a thrill!
Now try to roll it to the top,
Your lungs will burst, your eyes will pop!

Snowball the Snowman

BONGO & CONGO'S CHOCOLATE BANANAS

10 Servings

INGREDIENTS

- 5 bananas
- 10 ounces milk chocolate, chips
- 10 wooden popsicle sticks
- 1/2 cup chopped peanuts
- coconut
- rainbow sprinkles
- candy coated chocolate pieces

A FOOD TIP FROM NIP & ZIP

Nip's major recommendation about enjoying this frozen fruit temptation is to be absolutely 100% certain you have removed the entire banana peel. During the taste test, he observed Zip's lips slip off an unpeeled banana and Zip wound up accidentally kissing a stray alley cat.

HOW TO MAKE 'EM

♥ Place chopped peanuts and or any of the above coatings into shallow dishes. They can be mixed, or placed in separate plates.

♥ Put the chocolate pieces into a small microwavable bowl and microwave 1-2 minutes until all chocolate pieces are smooth. Be careful not to burn (this can also be done in a small saucepan on the stove, over very low heat. Stir constantly.) Remove from heat source.

♥ Peel the banana and cut in half. Push a wooden stick into the cut end of each banana half, inserting stick about half way.

♥ Using a spoon and rounded knife, spread chocolate all over the banana until completely coated. Immediately roll in the assorted toppings. Continue to do the same with each banana.

♥ Place the bananas on a waxed paper or plastic wrap lined plate. Put into the freezer, and freeze until firm. If you'd like to save for another day, wrap each banana in plastic wrap, and freeze.

Benny Beanie's™ Nutritional Facts (per serving):
Calories 259; Fat 13g (Saturated 16g); Cholesterol 6mg;
Sodium 58mg; Carbohydrate 31g; Protein 5g

One hot and humid afternoon
Bongo scampered around a lagoon,
While Congo hummed a banana tune
And acted like a big baboon!

Bongo the Monkey

Congo the Gorilla

CORAL'S TROPICAL DESSERT DRINK

2 Servings

INGREDIENTS

- 2   scoops sorbet or sherbert, any flavor
- 1   banana, peeled and sliced
- 1/2   cup strawberries, washed & sliced
- 1/2   cup blueberries, washed
- 1   12 oz. can ginger ale
- 2   long stemmed glasses

HOW TO MAKE 'EM

♥ Place 1 scoop of sorbet, (we like to use multi flavored sorbet) into each of two long stemmed glasses.

♥ Top with banana slices, strawberries and blueberries.

♥ Pour ginger ale over fruit.

♥ Decorate glass rim with a whole strawberry and paper umbrella.

A FOOD TIP FROM NIP & ZIP

Zip was doing chin-ups on the rungs of an antique chair (see 1998 Beanie Baby Handbook) and began to get a little dehydrated. Nip quickly came to his rescue with 8 fluid ounces of Coral's delicious elixir. "Sounds like a plan," moaned Zip. "Thanks."

Benny Beanie's*™ *Nutritional Facts (per serving):
Calories 222; Fat 1g (Saturated 0g); Cholesterol 0mg;
Sodium 20mg; Carbohydrate 53g; Protein 1g

Swimming through the coral reef
A boy or girl works up a thirst
For which there is one sure relief:
Puree de Coral, in one fast burst!

Coral the Fish

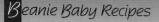
DAISY'S BLACK COW FLOAT

2 Servings

INGREDIENTS

- 1/2 pint vanilla ice cream
- 12 oz.root beer
  - whipped cream
  - cherry
- 2 tall glasses

HOW TO MAKE 'EM

♥ Place 1 scoop of vanilla ice cream into each of two tall glasses.

♥ Pour root beer over the ice cream, pouring slowly so the root beer does not spill over the top of the glass.

♥ Add another scoop of ice cream to the glass, if you have room.

♥ Put a long handled spoon and a straw into each glass. Top with whipped cream and a cherry.

♥ Makes two Black Cow floats.

A FOOD TIP FROM NIP & ZIP

This time it was Nip who got into trouble attempting to run the marathon on an empty stomach. Waiting along the sidelines to cheer him on, Zip was able to pass Nip a tall cool one with a straw as the crowd roared. Moral: Be prepared.

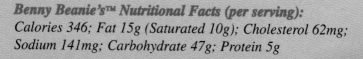

Benny Beanie's™ Nutritional Facts (per serving):
Calories 346; Fat 15g (Saturated 10g); Cholesterol 62mg;
Sodium 141mg; Carbohydrate 47g; Protein 5g

"Holy Cow!" we always say,
Especially on a summer day.
When heat exhaustion gets your goat
Be sure to down a Black Cow Float!

Daisy the Cow

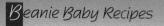
RAINBOW'S FRUIT KABOBS

15 Servings

INGREDIENTS

- 8 cups fruits, assorted, chunks
- 1 lemon
- 15 bamboo skewers
- 2 8 oz. packages cream cheese, softened
- 1 7 oz. jar marshmallow cream
- 1 8 oz. container strawberry yogurt

A FOOD TIP FROM NIP & ZIP

The cats rate this final (and classic) recipe as "A-1 refreshing and rejuvenating." They also recommend keeping fruit kabobs in the refrigerator (skip the insect-laden twigs) for an enervating shiver on the first bite, or lick. Two paws up!

HOW TO MAKE 'EM

♥ Cut up 8 cups of assorted fruits, such as apples, peaches, pears, bananas, orange sections, kiwis, strawberries, pineapple and/or grapes.

♥ For each kabob, dip apple, pear, banana and peach chunks into juice from 1 lemon, to prevent browning. Most other fruits will not need the lemon juice.

♥ Alternately thread the fruit on the skewers. Cover and chill until serving time.

♥ For dip, in a mixing bowl beat cream cheese and yogurt with an electric mixer on low speed until blended. This can be done by hand. Add the marshmallow cream, and mix until smooth. Cover the dip, and chill until serving time.

♥ To serve, arrange kabobs on a platter to resemble a rainbow. Serve with dip.

Benny Beanie's™ Nutritional Facts (per serving):
Calories 30; Fat 1g (Saturated 0g); Cholesterol 0mg;
Sodium 3mg; Carbohydrate 14g; Protein 1g

Although he wears an iguana's ridge,
Rainbow stocks his kitchen fridge
The way a smart chameleon should
With fruit kabobs and buggy wood.

Rainbow the Chameleon

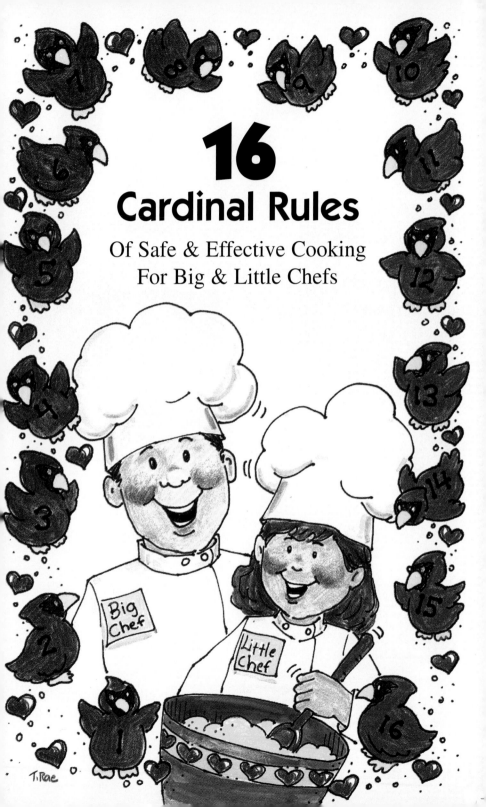

16
Cardinal Rules
Of Safe & Effective Cooking
For Big & Little Chefs

First, wash your hands well
before you start to cook.

Wear an apron
and tie back
your hair, if it
is long.

Read the recipe
completely before
you start cooking.

Arrange all of the ingredients
and cooking utensils you will
need.

5 Always keep paper towels or a sponge on hand in case you spill something.

 6 If you need to do any chopping, use a cutting board and a good knife with care and *adult supervision.*

If you are cooking on the stove, turn all handles to the side away from the heat to avoid knocking over. **7**

 8 Hold all hot dishes with pot holders and always place them on a trivet or stove top to avoid burning counter tops or table surfaces.

 Use large, heavy mixing bowls on a sturdy table to mix ingredients.

 If you are using an oven, have an adult turn it on about 15 minutes before using it. (This is called "pre-heating")

Always turn off the oven or the burner as soon as your dish is done.

 Presentation is very important – arrange your food with care and flair!

13 Place all cooking utensils in the sink and wash thoroughly.

Throw away any empty packages and refuse. **14**

15 Return all cooking ingredients and utensils to their proper places so they will be easy to locate the next time you cook.

16 Whatever recipe you decide to choose, *always* ask an adult to help you. Have fun!

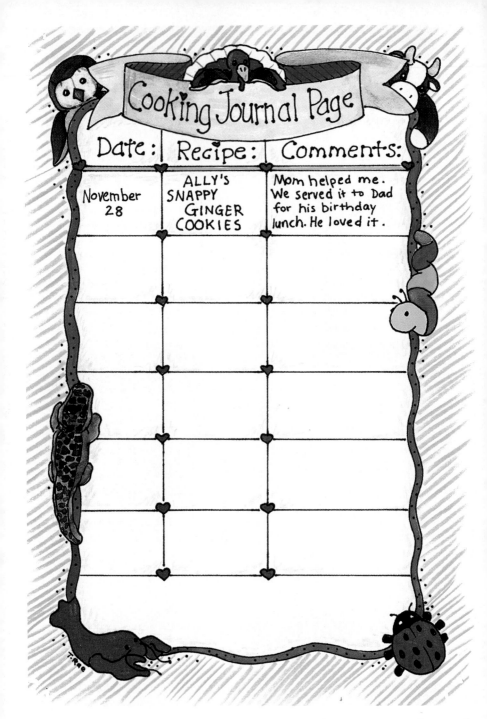

Cooking Journal Page

Date:	Recipe:	Comments:
November 28	ALLY'S SNAPPY GINGER COOKIES	Mom helped me. We served it to Dad for his birthday lunch. He loved it.

Make extra copies of this page. Make a construction paper cover then staple the pages into a booklet. Keep it with your cookbook. Each time you prepare a new recipe, record a notation in your Cooking Journal.

Gift Tag and Gift of Food

Here's what you need: construction paper, pencil, scissors, prepared recipe, paper punch, yarn or ribbon.

Here's what you do:

1. Prepare one of the Beanie Baby Cookbook recipes.
2. Trace the corresponding Beanie Baby onto paper and cut out the shape.
3. Print a special message and the recipe on the paper shape.
4. Punch a hole and string it to the prepared food.
5. Give it as a gift to a friend or neighbor.

to Grandma
Peanuts Peanutty
Cookies
from Jamie

Favorite Foods Survey

♥Breakfast Foods ♥

| pancakes | eggs + toast | cereal |

♥Snack Foods ♥

| popcorn | cheese + crackers | granola bars |

♥Dinner Foods ♥

| chicken | Pizza | hamburgers |

Ask friends and relatives which of the three foods they prefer for breakfast, snack, and dinner. Make a tally mark in the corresponding space for each answer they give. After surveying several people, compare the results of the information gathered.

Repeat the activity on another piece of paper incorporating other food choices, recipes from this book, or names of favorite restaurants.

APRON ART

Here's what you need: plain fabric apron (available at your local craft store), fabric paints.

Here's what you do:

1. Use fabric paints to draw pictures of your favorite Beanie Babies on the apron.
2. Print each Beanie Baby's name on the apron.
3. Print "Beanie Chef" across the front of the apron.
4. Wear the apron every time you prepare a Beanie recipe from this book.

Printing in Pudding

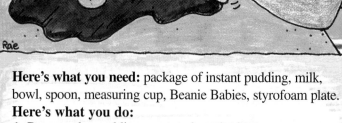

T. Rae

Here's what you need: package of instant pudding, milk, bowl, spoon, measuring cup, Beanie Babies, styrofoam plate.

Here's what you do:

1. Prepare the pudding as stated on the box.
2. Drop a dollop of firm pudding onto a clean table top, or styrofoam plate.
3. Write a Beanie Baby's name in the pudding.
4. Smooth over the name and lick your fingers.
5. Repeat steps three and four several times, writing a variety of Beanie Baby names.

Here's what you need: ten assorted and unusual tools or utensils from your kitchen drawers, slips of paper, pencil.

Here's what you do:

1. Display the items on the kitchen table.
2. Label each item with a number between one and ten.
3. Invite some friends over. Have them number their paper from one to ten.
4. Instruct them to observe and identify the various items, then write the name of each item or what it is used for, next to the corresponding number on the paper.

Suggested items to display: orange peeler, pastry blender, melon baller, cheese slicer, spaghetti spoon, frosting spreader, carrot crimper, apple corer/slicer, nut cracker, cake tester, orange juicer, wire wisk, vegetable brush, potato masher, meat tenderizing mallet.

FAMILY TIME

This is our family with our favorite Beanie Babies.

(draw here)

Our favorite meal to eat together is _____ _____.

Beanie Baby Apron Pattern

tie at neck

Add 2 inches here

Add 2 inches here

Make mine tie-dyed.

tie around waist

Add 3 inches here

Add 3 inches here

T.Rae

Sly

Patti

Trace this shape onto paper then cut out the shape. Add two inches to the length of each apron string as stated. Pin the pattern to fabric or felt then cut out an apron. Tie the apron to a Beanie Baby. Make an apron for several of your Beanie Babies. Have them wear their aprons when you're cooking in the kitchen.

Word/Object Matching Game

Here's what you need: 20 3x5 note cards, marker, twenty objects from the kitchen, two Beanie Babies.

Here's what you do:
1. Print the name of each kitchen item on a note card.
2. Display the kitchen items on the floor or table.
3. Stack the word cards face down on the table.
4. Have the two Beanie Babies take turns, turning over a card, reading the word, then matching the word with the kitchen item.
5. Play until all word cards have been matched.

Here's what you need: assortment of small kitchen utensils, cookie sheet, several Beanie Babies, paper, pencils.

Here's what you do:
1. Arrange the Beanie Babies and utensils on the cookie sheet.
2. Show the tray to some friends or family members for about thirty seconds.
3. Remove the tray from sight. Have the people write down as many of the items and Beanie Babies as they remember seeing on the tray.
4. Show the tray again. See who remembered the most.

T. Rae

Beanie Baby RESTAURANT

Here's what you need: table service for four, four Beanie Babies, 4 mini-menus, note pad, pencil. *Make mini menus by folding each notecard in half. Print "menu" on the cover then print an assortment of foods and prices on the inside of each menu.

Here's what you do:
1. Place the Beanie Babies at the table.
2. Pretend to be the waiter or waitress.
3. Hand each Beanie Baby a menu. Explain the "daily specials".
4. Take orders on the note pad then serve "pretend" meals to the Beanie Babies.

Sample dialogue: Welcome to our restaurant. Our daily specials today are... Would you care for anything to drink while you're looking at the menu? etc.

Here's what you need: an assortment of mini toy kitchen items *use those from Barbie doll or other toy sets, aprons from activity on page 201.

Here's what you do:
1. Put an apron on each Beanie Baby.
2. Have the Beanie Babies prepare several recipes using the miniature or toy kitchen materials.
3. Have the Beanie Babies serve each other.

Squealer says: Remember to eat foods from all four of the food groups each day.

Make a food group collage. Cut pictures of foods from magazines. Sort them into the four groups then paste them onto a sheet of construction paper. Hang this in your kitchen as a reminder to eat healthful foods. Draw a picture of Squealer at the center of the collage.

While waiting for your Beanie Baby recipe to cook...dance to your favorite Beanie Baby song!

Now Available On CD And Cassette!

Write your own recipe on this page.

_____'s recipe

for _____

Cooking Terms

Bake: Cooking food in the oven. Turn on the oven in advance so that it is at the right temperature, when you start baking.

Beat: Mix very fast with a spoon , an electric mixer, a whisk, or an egg beater.

Blend: Mix two or more ingredients together until smooth.

Boil: Cooking the liquid over high heat until bubbles keep rising, then break at the surface.

Broil: Cooking food by heat under a broiler in an electric or gas range.

Brown: Cook food until it starts to become a brown color on the outside.

Chill: Put food in the refrigerator to make it completely cold.

Chop: Using a sharp knife, (ask an adult to help with this) and a cutting board, or food processor, cut food into small uneven pieces. They don't have to be the same shape but they should be about the size of peas.

Coat: To cover food completely with an ingredient or food, such as flour, sauce or chocolate.

Combine: Mix ingredients together.

Condiment: A sauce or relish used to add flavor to food. For example; ketchup, mustard or worcestershire sauce .

Cool: Let the food stand on the counter until it is no longer hot. Food can be cooled more evenly and quickly by putting the food on a wire cooling rack.

Core: Cut out the stem end and remove the seeds.

Cover: Put plastic wrap, wax paper, foil or a lid over a dish of food to keep the air out. This helps to prevent food from becoming spoiled, or helps cook food faster when being cooked on a stove.

Crack an egg: Tap an uncooked egg with a table knife around the middle until it starts to crack, or tap it sharply against the side of a bowl. Over a bowl, pull the egg open with your thumbs, and let the egg yolk and white fall into the bowl. If any egg shell pieces fall into the bowl, remove them with a spoon.

Cream: To mix two or more ingredients until they are smooth, soft and well blended.

Dash/pinch: A very small amount of any ingredient – usually less than 1/8 teaspoon. To add a dash just sprinkle a little in your hand, and add to the food. A dash usually means liquid, and a pinch is usually dry ingredients.

De-vein: To remove the vein that runs down the back of a shrimp. Hold the shrimp, curve side up with one hand and slit the curve open with a small paring knife, using the other hand, remove the black vein and throw out.

Dice: Cut into cubes smaller than 1 inch. First slice the food then cut the slices into thin strips, turn and cut into small cubes.

Dissolve: Stir a dry ingredient (like flour) into a liquid (like water) until it disappears.

Double boiler, cook in: Fill the bottom of a double boiler (sauce pan) with about 2" of water. Set double boiler top (a metal bowl), containing food, in place over the hot water and cover. Bring water to a boil, then cook as directed. Often reduced to a lower temperature while cooking.

Drain: Put food in a colander or sieve so that the liquid separates from the solid portion, or just pour off liquid from a food.

Drizzle: Make something wet by sprinkling small drops over it.

Fold: Gently turn one part of a mixture over the other.

Fry: Cook in hot oil or butter.

Garnish: To decorate food to make it look interesting and attractive to the eye.

Grate: To rub food, like a block of cheese against a grater to cut into small pieces.

Grease: Spread bottom and sides of pan or cookie sheet with butter (place some butter on a piece of waxed paper or plastic wrap.)

Grind: To make food into tiny particles using a food processor, grinder or blender.

Grill: Cook food on a rack over coals.

Knead: Place the dough on a counter, use your hands to push against the dough. Then fold the dough, turn it and push against it again to make smooth.

Line: Cover a pan or cookie sheet with paper to prevent food from sticking.

Mash: Soften and beak apart with a fork.

Marinate: To place food in a liquid so it will become tender and very flavorful. Do not reuse marinade that have been used for meat, poultry or fish.

Measure: A specific amount of an ingredient using measuring tools, such as cups and spoons.

Melt: Heat a solid until it becomes a liquid.

Mince: Chop into tiny pieces.

Mix: To combine ingredients with a stirring motion, using a fork, spoon or a blender.

Peel: Cut off the skin with a knife or peel with your finger.

Preheat: To turn on the oven about 15 minutes before using, setting to the desired temperature.

Prick: To pierce food, such as a potato, so it won't explode, rise, expand or shrink as it cooks. Using fork tines is recommended for piercing a potato, before baking.

Shred: Rub an ingredient across a shredder to make large pieces. (Shredding cheese for example for Lucky's pizza.)

Sifting: To sift flour, or confectioners sugar, shake it through a sieve. This gets rid of lumps, and makes the flour or sugar light and airy.

Skillet: A name for a frying pan. There are many types of skillets. When a recipe does not indicate otherwise, you may use any all purpose skillet.

Slice: Using a sharp knife (ask an adult for help) and a cutting board, hold the food firmly on the board, cut a thin piece off the end. Continue doing this until all of the food is cut into pieces about the same size.

Stir: To combine ingredients with a spoon, using a circular motion.

Strain: To separate solids from liquids through a strainer or fine sieve.

Stuff: To fill a cavity with food with a mixture of ingredients. (Puffer's Puffy Potatoes)

Toast: To brown food by the indirect heat of an oven (toasting nuts for Speedy's Turtle recipe for example) or by direct heat of a broiler.

Toss: Mix ingredients lightly in a bowl by lifting them with two spoons, two forks or your hands. (Twigs' Tree Top Salad)

Turn: To move the dish halfway around so that the food cooks more evenly. This is used in the microwave for foods that can not be stirred.

Whip: To beat using a beater or whisk. Whipping mixes in ingredients quickly to add to increase volume and lighten the mixture.

Whisk: To whisk food, beat lightly and quickly with a metal whisk or electric mixer.

Beanie Baby Birthdays

Were You Born on the Same Day as a Beanie?

New May 30th Releases in Red

JANUARY

Jan. 3, 1993	Spot
Jan. 5, 1997	Kuku
Jan. 6, 1993	Patti
Jan. 13, 1996	Crunch
Jan. 14, 1997	Spunky
Jan. 15, 1996	Mel
Jan. 18, 1994	Bones
Jan. 21, 1996	Nuts
Jan. 25, 1995	Peanut
Jan. 26, 1996	Chip

FEBRUARY

Feb. 1, 1996	Peace
Feb. 4, 1997	Fetch
Feb. 13, 1995	Stinky
Feb. 13, 1995	Pinky
Feb. 14, 1994	Valentino
Feb. 17, 1996	Baldy
Feb. 20, 1996	Roary
Feb. 22, 1995	Tank
Feb. 25, 1994	Happy
Feb. 27, 1996	Sparky
Feb. 28, 1995	Flip

MARCH

Mar. 2, 1995	Coral
Mar. 6, 1994	Nip
Mar. 8, 1996	Doodle
Mar. 8, 1996	Strut
Mar. 12, 1997	Rocket
Mar. 14, 1994	Ally
Mar. 19, 1996	Seaweed
Mar. 20, 1997	Early
Mar. 21, 1996	Fleece
Mar. 28, 1994	Zip

APRIL

Apr. 3, 1996	Hoppity
Apr. 4, 1997	Hissy
Apr. 5, 1997	Whisper
Apr. 7, 1997	Gigi
Apr. 12, 1996	Curly
Apr. 16, 1997	Jake
Apr. 18, 1995	Ears
Apr. 19, 1994	Quackers
Apr. 23, 1993	Squealer
Apr. 25, 1993	Legs
Apr. 27, 1993	Chocolate

MAY

May 1, 1995	Lucky
May 1, 1996	Wrinkles
May 2, 1996	Pugsly
May 3, 1996	Chops
May 10, 1994	Daisy
May 11, 1995	Lizzy
May 13, 1993	Flash
May 15, 1995	Snort
May 19, 1995	Twigs
May 21, 1994	Mystic
May 28, 1996	Floppity
May 30, 1996	Rover
May 31, 1997	Wise

JUNE

June 1, 1996	Hippity
June 3, 1996	Freckles
June 5, 1997	Tracker
June 8, 1995	Bucky
June 8, 1995	Manny
June 11, 1995	Stripes
June 15, 1996	Scottie
June 17, 1996	Gracie
June 19, 1993	Pinchers
June 27, 1995	Bessie

JULY

July 1, 1996	Scoop
July 1, 1996	Maple
July 2, 1995	Bubbles
July 4, 1996	Lefty
July 4, 1996	Righty
July 4, 1997	Glory
July 8, 1993	Splash
July 14, 1995	Ringo
July 15, 1994	Blackie
July 19, 1995	Grunt
July 20, 1995	Weenie

AUGUST

Aug. 1, 1995	Garcia
Aug. 9, 1995	Hoot
Aug. 12, 1997	Iggy
Aug. 13, 1996	Spike
Aug. 14, 1994	Speedy
Aug. 17, 1995	Bongo
Aug. 23, 1995	Digger
Aug. 27, 1995	Sting
Aug. 28, 1997	Pounce

SEPTEMBER

Sept. 3, 1995	Inch
Sept. 3, 1996	Claude
Sept. 5, 1995	Magic
Sept. 9, 1997	Bruno
Sept. 12, 1996	Sly
Sept. 16, 1995	Kiwi
Sept. 16, 1995	Derby
Sept. 18, 1995	Tusk
Sept. 21, 1997	Stretch
Sept. 29, 1997	Stinger

OCTOBER

Oct. 1, 1997	Smoochy
Oct. 3, 1996	Bernie
Oct. 9, 1996	Doby
Oct. 10, 1997	Jabber
Oct. 12, 1996	Tuffy
Oct. 14, 1997	Rainbow
Oct. 16, 1995	Bumble
Oct. 17, 1996	Dotty
Oct. 22, 1996	Snip
Oct. 28, 1996	Spinner
Oct. 30, 1995	Radar
Oct. 29, 1996	Batty
Oct. 31, 1995	Spooky

NOVEMBER

Nov. 3, 1997	Puffer
Nov. 6, 1996	Pouch
Nov. 7, 1997	Ants
Nov. 9, 1996	Congo
Nov. 14, 1993	Cubbie
Nov. 14, 1994	Goldie
Nov. 20, 1997	Prance
Nov. 21, 1996	Nanook
Nov. 27, 1996	Gobbles
Nov. 28, 1995	Teddy Brown
Nov. 29, 1994	Inky

DECEMBER

Dec. 2, 1996	Jolly
Dec. 6, 1997	Fortune
Dec. 8, 1996	Waves
Dec. 12, 1996	Blizzard
Dec. 14, 1996	Seamore
Dec. 16, 1995	Velvet
Dec. 19, 1995	Waddle
Dec. 21, 1996	Echo
Dec. 22, 1996	Snowball
Dec. 24, 1995	Ziggy
Dec. 25, 1996	'97 Teddy

Beanie Baby

Kid Beanie™

BLACK = Current   RED = Retired

Name	Cost $	Name	Cost $	Name	Cost $
❏ Ally		❏ Doodle		❏ Kuku (5/98)	
❏ Ants (5/98)		❏ Dotty		❏ Lefty	
❏ Baldy		❏ Early (5/98)		❏ Legs	
❏ Batty		❏ Ears		❏ Libearty	
❏ Bernie		❏ Echo		❏ Lizzy-Tie-Dyed	
❏ Bessie		❏ Fetch (5/98)		❏ Lizzy-Blue	
❏ Blackie		❏ Flash		❏ Lucky-7	
❏ Blizzard		❏ Fleece		❏ Lucky-11	
❏ Bones		❏ Flip		❏ Lucky-21	
❏ Bongo-Dk Tail		❏ Floppity		❏ Magic	
❏ Bongo-Lt Tail		❏ Flutter		❏ Manny	
❏ Britannia		❏ Fortune (5/98)		❏ Maple	
❏ Bronty		❏ Freckles		❏ Mel	
❏ Brownie		❏ Garcia		Mystic	
❏ Bruno		❏ Gigi (5/98)		❏ Fine Yarn	
❏ Bubbles		❏ Glory (5/98)		❏ Tan Horn	
❏ Bucky		❏ Gobbles		❏ Striped Horn	
❏ Bumble		❏ Goldie		❏ Nana (Bongo)	
❏ Caw		❏ Gracie		❏ Nanook	
❏ Chilly		❏ Grunt		❏ Nip-Large	
❏ Chip		❏ Happy-Grey		❏ Nip-All Gold	
❏ Chocolate		❏ Happy-Lav		❏ Nip-White Paws	
❏ Chops		❏ Hippity		❏ Nuts	
❏ Claude		❏ Hissy		❏ Patti-Maroon	
❏ Congo		❏ Hoot		❏ Patti-Purple	
❏ Coral		❏ Hoppity		❏ Peace	
❏ Crunch		❏ Humphrey		Peanut	
❏ Cubbie		❏ Iggy		❏ Royal Blue	
❏ Curly		❏ Inch-Felt		❏ Light Blue	
❏ Daisy		❏ Inch-Wool		❏ Peking	
❏ Derby-Fine		❏ Inky-Tan		❏ Pinchers	
❏ Derby-Coarse		❏ Inky-Pink		❏ Pinky	
❏ Derby-Spot		❏ Jabber (5/98)		❏ Pouch	
❏ Digger-Orange		❏ Jake (5/98)		❏ Pounce	
❏ Digger-Red		❏ Jolly		❏ Prance	
❏ Doby		❏ Kiwi		❏ Pride	

214

Checklist

How many of the 197 Beanie Babies listed below do you have in your collection?

BLACK = Current   RED = Retired

Name	Cost $	Name	Cost $	Name	Cost $
❑ Princess		❑ Sting		❑ Waves	
❑ Puffer		❑ Stinger (5/98)		❑ Web	
❑ Pugsley		❑ Stinky		❑ Weenie	
❑ Punchers		❑ Stretch		❑ Whisper (5/98)	
❑ Quacker-No Wings		❑ Stripes-Dark		❑ Wise (5/98)	
❑ Quackers-Wings		❑ Stripes-Fuzzy		❑ Wrinkles	
❑ Radar		❑ Stripes-Light		❑ Ziggy	
❑ Rainbow		❑ Strut		❑ Zip-Large	
❑ Rex		❑ Tabasco		❑ Zip-All Black	
❑ Righty		❑ Tank-7 Plates		❑ Zip-White Paws	
❑ Ringo		❑ Tank-9 Plates		**1998 Teenie Beanies**	
❑ Roary		❑ Tank-9 Pits (sm)		❑ Bones	
❑ Rocket (5/98)		❑ 1997 Teddy		❑ Bongo	
❑ Rover		Teddy (Old Face)		❑ Doby	
❑ Scoop		❑ Brown		❑ Happy	
❑ Scottie		❑ Cranberry		❑ Inch	
❑ Seamore		❑ Jade		❑ Mel	
❑ Seaweed		❑ Magenta		❑ Peanut	
❑ Slither		❑ Teal		❑ Pinchers	
❑ Sly-Brown Belly		❑ Violet		❑ Scoop	
❑ Sly-White Belly		Teddy (New Face)		❑ Twigs	
❑ Smoochy		❑ Brown		❑ Waddle	
❑ Snip		❑ Cranberry		❑ Zip	
❑ Snort		❑ Jade		**1997 Teenie Beanies**	
❑ Snowball		❑ Magenta		❑ Chocolate	
❑ Sparky		❑ Teal		❑ Chops	
❑ Speedy		❑ Violet		❑ Goldie	
❑ Spike		❑ Violet (Ty Reps)		❑ Lizz	
❑ Spinner		❑ Tracker (5/98)		❑ Patti	
❑ Splash		❑ Trap		❑ Pinky	
❑ Spooky		❑ Tuffy		❑ Quacks	
❑ Spot-No Spot		❑ Tusk		❑ Seamore	
❑ Spot-w/Spot		❑ Twigs		❑ Snort	
❑ Spunky		❑ Valentino		❑ Speedy	
❑ Squealer		❑ Velvet			
❑ Steg		❑ Waddle			

The Answer Page

Professor Beanie™

Professor Beanie's Food Riddles
(from page 6)

1. Because he was very hungry!

2. Snip.

3. Jolly Ranchers.

4. Tabasco!

5. They asked him to shell out the money.

6. Lefty and Righty.

7. Peanut, silly!

8. Blueberry stain remover.

9. Because good manners are not extinct.

10. Spike.

Help Roary And Friends Find The Hidden Objects
(from page 8)

" MY MOM SAYS I CANT KEEP BUYING AND SELLING BEANIE BABIES ON THE NET, IT WOULD PUSH US INTO A HIGHER TAX BRACKET !!!"